Advance ... for
You Are a Data Person

"As Amelia Parnell states in her opening—it is clear the analytics revolution is here. The timing of this revolution will be critical to higher education's efforts to design programs and student success initiatives that are data-driven and data-informed. Parnell's book is both comprehensive and accessible for faculty and staff who are leading this revolution."—*Kevin Kruger, President/ CEO, NASPA–Student Affairs Administrators in Higher Education*

"In *You Are a Data Person: Strategies for Using Analytics on Campus*, Amelia Parnell reassures her readers what we all suspected and secretly hoped to be true—each and every one of us possesses a data identity and now is the opportune moment in higher education to take ownership. From interviews with experts and scholars in the field to illustrative case studies, the author provides a vision and road map for how we can all benefit from and contribute to this mission."—*Helen L. Chen, Research Scientist, Designing Education Lab, Department of Mechanical Engineering, Stanford University; Executive Committee, Association for Authentic Experiential Evidence-Based Learning*

"Amelia Parnell deftly navigates not only the current state of data proliferation and its impact on professionals across campuses, but also points readers toward the future of data use and collaboration for improving the student experience. This book is essential reading for individuals and institutions looking to harness the power of data to optimize the college experience for students in a holistic way."—*Bethany Miller, Director of Institutional Research, Macalester College*

"*You Are a Data Person: Strategies for Using Analytics on Campus* should be required reading for anyone who works on a college campus. This book is the not-so-gentle nudge that every college faculty and staff member needs: a reminder that each of us has a data identity, no matter our role or place in an organizational chart. More important, it's a reminder that we have agency to make a real difference in the lives of our students by making more data-informed decisions. Against the backdrop of COVID recovery and renewed calls for racial justice, Dr. Parnell's book couldn't come at a better time." —*Archie P. Cubarrubia, Former Vice Provost for Institutional Effectiveness, Miami Dade College*

"To those who see the application of institutional data as a daunting black box, Parnell offers an accessible, practical way in. She begins with strengths and encourages a growth mindset – familiar strategies for most educators, but applied to ourselves. And best of all, her categorization of data temperaments suggests a way to build diverse, effective project teams, leveraging the social ways we learn and work together."—*Ken O'Donnell, Vice Provost, California State University Dominguez Hills*

YOU ARE A DATA PERSON

YOU ARE A DATA PERSON

Strategies for Using Analytics on Campus

Amelia Parnell

Foreword by Robert A. Schwartz

STERLING, VIRGINIA

Published by Stylus Publishing, LLC.
22883 Quicksilver Drive
Sterling, Virginia 20166-2019

Library of Congress Cataloging-in-Publication Data
Copyright data for this volume has been applied for

13-digit ISBN: 978-1-64267-136-0 (cloth)
13-digit ISBN: 978-1-64267-137-7 (paperback)
13-digit ISBN: 978-1-64267-138-4 (library networkable e-edition)
13-digit ISBN: 978-1-64267-139-1 (consumer e-edition)

Printed in the United States of America

All first editions printed on acid-free paper
that meets the American National Standards Institute
Z39-48 Standard.

Bulk Purchases
Quantity discounts are available for use in workshops and
for staff development.
Call 1-800-232-0223

First Edition, 2021

I dedicate this book to everyone with whom I've had a data-related conversation. Your energy and interest motivated me to create this resource to help us address our biggest higher education challenges together.

CONTENTS

At the risk of dating both of us, I recall very vividly one of my first encounters with a new graduate student a "few" years ago named Amelia Parnell. I was teaching an advanced graduate seminar on the literature review, often chapter 2 in most doctoral dissertations. I recall being surprised at the time, as Amelia was still early in her doctoral program. When I questioned her about taking the course too early, she responded with what I would learn was her typical enthusiasm, "Oh, I really want to take the course—I want to learn how to do the research now!"

It is no surprise that Parnell would choose to write and engage other professionals in sharing her long and successful engagement with data, research, and the process of learning how to get "it" right. Amelia has emerged as a national figure in data collection, analysis, and reporting through her time as a vice president for research and policy for NASPA–Student Affairs Administrators in Higher Education. She has compiled a book that reflects her commitment to data and research and done it in a very accessible and attractive way. This book should be a singular source of information, advice, and support to anyone who needs greater interaction with data and its application—which at this point in the 21st century means all of us.

The great value of this book is that the author is not reliant on only her own point of view or preferences. Instead, she has reached out to many others who are engaged in data collection, analysis, and application and asked for their advice and recommendations. Indeed, this book represents interviews and discussions with 40 professionals from a very broad sample of experts, both scholars and practitioners. By distilling the knowledge and experiences of others, this book provides the best advice currently available on how to become a data driven person at several different levels. Using the self-assessment process outlined in the book, anyone from an early entrant into the "world" of data acquisition and analysis to the "seasoned" professional can find something of value and real benefit to their understanding and application of data, data collection, data analysis, and data forecasting.

Amelia speaks with confidence and competence as someone who has been a researcher at the state and national levels, who has taught successfully at the graduate level, and who has led at the national level in identifying and managing some of the critical questions of our time. The future is clearly going to rely on the effective use of data and data users to help us shape the world we live in. This book is and will be a valuable asset in that effort.

I am excited and honored to help introduce Amelia Parnell's latest venture to the world and wish her continued success, boundless energy (which she has already), and a very wide readership for this useful and valuable take on data, its value, and effective use. She has and will continue to earn gratitude, respect, and appreciation for her commitment to helping others learn and understand what some may see as the daunting world of data collection, analysis, and application. She knows very well how data, research, and policy at all levels can improve not only what we know but how we can use data successfully to achieve our goals.

Robert A. Schwartz
Professor, Higher Education
Educational Leadership and Policy Studies
Florida State University
Tallahassee, FL

PREFACE

There is ample evidence to confirm that the analytics revolution is here, and it connects to nearly every industry across the world. For example, it is now commonplace for consumer products such as watches to gather data about one's heart rate and sleep patterns. Navigation systems can provide the best routes for travel based on real-time traffic patterns. Companies are now using more sophisticated advertising approaches that include data about buyers' prior purchases. The field of higher education is also using such tailored data approaches to serve individuals. Many of today's students are accustomed to having information readily available to them and, as a result, colleges and universities are in need of new strategies for harnessing the increased demand for data. In this analytics revolution, institutions are striving to deliver the optimal college experience for students while balancing varying needs, resources, and priorities. This is a good opportunity for professionals to expand their understanding of the data to which they have access. In essence, this is a good time for all professionals to embrace and build upon their data identity.

Many publications on topics related to data and analytics address why this is a pivotal time for more professionals to make data-informed decisions. However, such publications are often regarded as being primarily for audiences of professionals with roles of data scientist, institutional researcher, or analyst. As a result, there appears to be a gap in available literature that illuminates how data roles are not limited to certain professional titles. In fact, current higher education trends suggest that every function on a campus would benefit from a more strategic use of data. *You Are a Data Person: Strategies for Using Analytics on Campus* introduces the data identity framework, a composition of six categories of skills and abilities that every professional likely possesses to some degree. The purpose of the framework is to help readers understand their strongest data-related skills and abilities and how to use them to contribute to data-informed activities.

This book differs from other data-related resources because it is informed by 40 interviews with higher education professionals with varying levels of responsibility and experience. When asked about various portions of the data identity framework, the professionals' responses confirmed that while everyone has a different mix of abilities, each person has something valuable to offer. This book is intended to inspire readers to learn about their data identity and use it to collaborate with others. Each chapter provides reflections from professionals about their current challenges with using data and their goals for using data in the future. Although some professionals expressed concerns about how campuses will be able to manage the ever-changing data climate, nearly every person provided an example of something good that has occurred in the past year from their intentional use of data. These findings suggest that while challenges remain, campuses will continue to foster a less segmented data environment, one in which professionals work across departments and functions to deliver the best possible experience for students.

This book is framed by two assumptions that are woven through each section. The first is that every higher education professional, regardless of their role, can find a use for data in their daily work. The second is that the most ideal climate for successful data work is one that promotes open communication, supportive sharing of progress and results, and ongoing collaboration. It is reasonable to expect that these assumptions are aspirational for some campuses, especially those that have not fully developed a high-functioning and strategic use of data across divisions and functions. However, these two assumptions are attainable because both rely on the power of community, which is a strong lever for helping any campus reach its data goals.

Every higher education professional, regardless of their role, can find a use for data in their daily work.

The field of higher education is currently experiencing significant shifts that are requiring professionals to reconsider, refine, and restructure their work. Three such shifts are related to the provision of programs and services to students, the delivery of integrated learning experiences, and the forecasting and management of enrollment. For example, the rising cost to deliver high-quality programs and services to students has pushed many institutions to reallocate resources to find efficiencies. Also, more institutions are intentionally connecting classroom and cocurricular learning experiences which, in some instances, requires an increased gathering of evidence that students have acquired certain skills and competencies. In addition to programs, services, and pedagogy, professionals are constantly monitoring the rates at which students are entering, remaining enrolled in, and leaving the institution, as those movements impact the institution's financial position. It is for these reasons and more that higher education professionals will need to consistently approach their work with a data-informed perspective.

The U.S. Department of Education (ED) currently requires institutions that participate in or are applicants for participation in any federal financial assistance program authorized by Title IV of the Higher Education Act of 1965 to complete all surveys for the Integrated Postsecondary Education Data System (IPEDS; National Center for Education Statistics, n.d.). Many campuses have an office of institutional research (IR) or, at a minimum, an individual responsible for managing compliance with IPEDS data reporting and other types of mandatory data collection. In 1965, the Association for Institutional Research was formed to provide professional development for institutional researchers and to foster community among those who have data responsibilities. Since that time, both the function of institutional research and the IR profession have expanded significantly. Today, institutional research includes many more types of data-related activities, and institutional researchers often collaborate with colleagues in other areas of the campus. As a result, many campuses are embracing a campus-wide culture of data use, and professionals, both in institutional research and in other areas, will need to increase their capacity to make data-informed decisions.

Swing et al. (2016) conducted a national survey of IR offices and found that the majority of institutions have an IR office with three or fewer staff. However, in many instances, this is not enough personnel capacity to address all of the campus data needs for two primary reasons. First, the IR office typically manages mandatory reporting, ad hoc data requests, and new campus-wide data projects. These responsibilities could easily consume most, if not all, of the campus IR office's resources. Second, there are dozens of campus functions that need to make data-informed decisions with information that is gathered and managed by professionals in the specific function rather than those in the IR office. For example, the library might need to compare the rates at which students visit the physical campus location to the rates at which students access the library remotely. Such information would likely be gathered by campus library personnel. Thus, those professionals should have the resources, preparation, and opportunity to analyze their own data.

Swing and Ross (2016) forecasted that in the years ahead, more campus professionals who are not working in IR offices will be users and stewards of data. Their work resulted in a *Statement of Aspirational Practice for Institutional Research*. The statement proposes that students, faculty, and staff are decision makers and that campuses should have a networked IR function, one in which data tools are available institution-wide, data literacy skills are required for all employees, and professionals have ongoing access to data-related training (Swing & Ross, 2016). In order for campuses to fully leverage data to make the best decisions possible, it is critical that everyone at the institution, regardless of their role, use data in their work. The goal of this type of dispersed analytics approach is not to remove or replace the work of

IR offices but instead to give every decision maker the tools and opportunity to work with the best information possible.

The most ideal climate for successful data work is one that promotes open communication, supportive sharing of progress and results, and ongoing collaboration.

Gagliardi and Turk (2017) suggest that one of the most important steps that can be taken to harness the analytics revolution is the development of an analytics culture that is widespread and positive. Such a climate fosters greater opportunities for colleagues across functions to successfully work together. This book proposes that to be an effective data user in a higher education environment, one must know and understand their institution's core priorities and existing processes, both of which provide the context for making sound decisions. Therefore, professionals should engage in both solo and collaborative data work. For example, many institutions have a student retention committee that is comprised of professionals from various campus offices such as IR, academic affairs, student affairs, and enrollment management. The committee is primarily focused on monitoring the rates at which students are on a path to earning a credential without major delays. When the committee discovers students who may need additional resources to complete their credential on time, the group uses data to determine next steps. These types of committees thrive when actions are aligned with the institution's priorities, and successful execution relies on a dispersed but connected approach, one in which everyone has a role, open communication is encouraged, and transparency is welcomed.

This book describes the current climate for data use in higher education with a focus on four priorities for the reader: (a) providing context for the range in levels at which professionals use data; (b) providing a framework to describe the various skills and abilities that comprise one's data identity; (c) offering tangible examples for how one can make data-informed contributions; and (d) inspiring readers to proactively engage in data projects. Professionals can refer to this book regularly, as it contains numerous references to existing literature, practical examples, and resources that cover an array of topics. For example, the data identity framework in chapter 2 and the accompanying self-assessment exercise in chapter 7 are useful resources to revisit every few years, especially as campus priorities change and individual roles and responsibilities evolve.

As internal and external pressure continues to mount for college professionals to provide evidence of successful activities, programs, and services, it is likely that nearly every campus professional will eventually need to approach their work with a data-informed perspective. The interview excerpts throughout the book are from professionals in a variety of campus functions, including but not limited to student affairs, academic affairs, institutional research, and enrollment management. The first section of this book offers a foundation by describing current trends, commonly used terms, and the data identity framework. The second section focuses on practical uses of data, including 20 examples of how to monitor programs, services, and students' progress. The book concludes with the self-assessment exercise and predictions about the future of data and analytics use in higher education.

ACKNOWLEDGMENTS

I thank God for giving me the ability to write this book. I am also very thankful for all of my family, friends, and colleagues for their love and support.

I appreciate all of the individuals who participated in background interviews and offered advice for this project. The on-the-ground examples from professionals who are currently working at institutions helped me make this a more timely and relevant resource. I want this book to present relatable perspectives, spur new conversations, and encourage more widespread collaboration. I sincerely believe that everyone has valuable data-related abilities and I hope this book inspires professionals to explore their data identity.

I thank Stylus Publishing for the opportunity to release this book and I am especially appreciative of David Brightman for his ongoing interest in my ideas about the current and future state of higher education. As I consider the many challenges and opportunities that the field will encounter in the years ahead, I am committed to using my voice to elevate practical strategies that can help us deliver the valuable college experiences that students seek and deserve.

AN OPTIMAL TIME
FOR DATA PEOPLE

There are a lot of people who are in the same boat. Use it as an opportunity to build connections and keep the lines of communication open. We get to that point sometimes when we are afraid to ask for help. We are afraid to say this is not working. Try to reach out to get the help you might need.

—Amanda Propst Cuevas, Florida Atlantic University

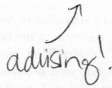

advising!

This is an optimal time for the advice offered in the previous quote (A.P. Cuevas, personal communication, January 3, 2020). It is timely because most institutions are allocating more financial resources to prioritize the use of data. For example, as shown in Figure 1.1 as follows, Parnell et al. (2018) surveyed institutions of varying sizes and sectors and found that nearly 90% were investing in data and analytics

Figure 1.1. Institutions' investment in data and analytics.

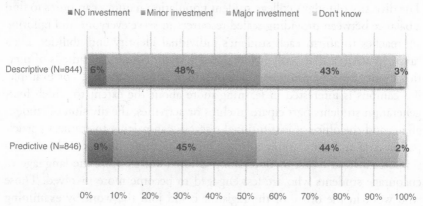

Source: Parnell et al. (2018).

projects. This implies that regardless of the type of campus for which most professionals work, there exists an environment in which the focus on data is visible.

This high level of investment in data and analytics creates more opportunities for professionals across the campus to collaborate. There are countless ways that campuses can use data and, among those, five primary ones are good for professionals to focus their effort. These five uses are to support the institution's mission; affirm students' abilities; identify opportunities to work efficiently; connect projects across offices and departments; and celebrate successful efforts.

Supporting the Campus Mission

An institution's mission is a statement of how the campus intends to serve students, engage with the community and external partners, and contribute to the higher education industry. Thus, professionals who seek a broader purpose for making data-informed decisions can first consider how their work supports the campus mission. For example, if an institution's mission is to provide a high-quality educational experience for commuter students, a person who works in parking services can contribute by analyzing the extent to which parking is available during peak times of the day. By ensuring that parking challenges are minimal, the professional is supporting the campus mission in a meaningful way.

Affirming Students' Abilities

The diversity of today's college student population requires campuses to find a balance between providing scaled resources to serve everyone and tailoring approaches to affirm each student's individual identity and abilities. Data can help achieve that goal, as integrated systems connect hundreds of metrics about students' progress, including their routine actions. For example, if a campus is interested in learning more about the extent to which first-generation students participate in clubs or activities, the division of student affairs and the office of institutional research can partner to connect participation data and demographic data. Communications professionals can also support such an effort by developing tailored and appropriate language to encourage students who are less engaged to become more involved. Those who work in the office of the registrar could join the work by examining ways to officially document evidence of students' cocurricular achievements.

Identifying Efficiencies

The introduction to this book referenced a theme of collaboration, which certainly relates to goals of efficiency. In fact, as shown in Figure 1.2 as follows, in their study of institutions' use of data for student success, Parnell et al. (2018) also found that more than 70% of campuses have a goal of conducting studies to more efficiently deliver programs and services. For example, advising is a critical type of support for many college students. Whether the advice needed is academic, financial, or career related, it is important that students receive the support that will help them make their best decisions. It is common for advising functions to be both centralized and decentralized, which results in an even greater need for efficient delivery of advising resources. As faculty, staff, and administrators collaborate to give students timely advice, their use of data is integral to students' overall success at the institution.

Figure 1.2. Institutions' goals for conducting student success studies (N=389).

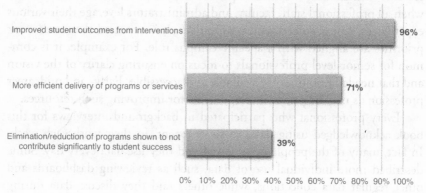

Source: Parnell et al. (2018).

Connecting Projects Across Departments

As suggested in the opening quote, a collaborative environment is ideal for campus-wide data efforts. Everyone has a different set of skills and abilities, which is a good reason for professionals to create and maintain connections to colleagues in other offices. For example, many institutions now provide emergency aid to help students who experience an unexpected hardship. In order to deliver the aid to students in a short amount of time, professionals in the financial aid office often work with colleges from other areas such as student affairs. These departments can work together to not only ensure that students receive emergency help but additional follow-up support as well. Some campuses are using data to inform strategic scaling of emergency aid efforts, such as proactively communicating with students about the availability of the aid.

[handwritten note: fine line b/n → celebrate + excess accountability]

Celebrating Successful Efforts

Data-informed celebrations can be campus-wide, such as a periodic newsletter to the community that describes the positive impact of more students becoming engaged in on-campus work opportunities. Department-level celebrations are just as important, as colleagues can use data to showcase improvements in service delivery. For example, a campus health and fitness center might have data that show both an increase in the rates at which students visit the facility and a declining average wait time to use various equipment and other resources.

The introduction also referenced a theme of everyone finding a use for data in their daily work. Campuses are most productive and successful when all professional staff, faculty, and administrators leverage their various experiences, competencies, and perspectives. It is expected that one's work priorities are aligned with a specific campus role. For example, it is common for senior-level professionals to focus on ensuring clarity of the vision and that needed resources are available and accessible. Early- and midcareer professionals may be primarily responsible for improving such resources.

Every professional who participated in background interviews for this book acknowledged using data, to some extent, in their work each week. In fact, many of the people interviewed said they use data every day. Some described more individual use of data, such as reviewing dashboards and other regular data collections, while others said they discuss data during recurring meetings with colleagues. All of the interviews confirmed that frequent data use is helpful, and the following quote from Darryl Holloman at Spelman College (personal communication, November 4, 2019) describes this level of action well:

> I would say basically every day of the week you are analyzing data that, in some regard, is having an impact on the work. Every day we are looking at numbers to make sure that we are having an impact on the larger mission of the institution. For example, a slight drop of enrollment by say 35 students at some institutions could equate to one million dollars. This type of drop in enrollment could directly impact the ability of the college to support programs, services and activities that advance retention initiatives.

The background interviews revealed routine use of several types of data and information, including but not limited to financial metrics, enrollment projections, and student learning outcomes. Those who said they use data daily emphasized the need to have real-time access to information, because their resulting decisions often impact students and operations. For example, one respondent who serves as the chair of an academic department said that the role requires close attention to the budget, particularly where to invest resources to both continue current program offerings and determine which courses should be offered in the semesters ahead. These examples confirm that professionals have the kind of multifaceted data identity that chapter 2 will describe.

Successful institutions rely on professionals from every area to make data-informed decisions. For example, the Association for Institutional Research's jobs board website routinely lists dozens of advertisements for data-related positions across the United States. Such positions range in level of responsibility and years of relevant experience. Roles such as analyst, researcher, and data scientist, as well as titles such as coordinator, director, and senior director, are abundant in the listings (Association for Institutional Research, 2020). These job postings are not limited to offices of institutional research and include many other campus functions as well, which signals the value of using data in one's daily work. The following quote from Marina Macomber at Northeastern University (personal communication, November 22, 2019) is a good description of a campus-wide approach to using data analytics:

> At our university, our senior leadership is extremely data driven. We have been trained year over year about building a case and using data to tell the story. Northeastern, campus wide, not just student affairs, is a heavily data-driven university. That is the culture here by far. Assessments have always been a priority and then looking at the data, understanding the story it tells us, and making changes or informed decisions based on the data. So, the clearer the story that we can tell with data, the more successful we are.

While many professionals have completed a formal course related to statistics, mathematics, or research, some are in need of additional professional development that is focused on practical methodologies and specific analyses. Such preparation should also help professionals understand frequently used terms. The following explanations are not intended to be the sole or definitive description of each term but instead an easy-to-understand synopsis for the everyday data user. The terms are organized into three categories: foundational words; methods and tools; and structures and rules.

Foundational Words

Algorithm. A step-by-step process, often completed by a computer, which is used to solve a mathematical problem. With regard to higher education, algorithms are sometimes used to predict future student outcomes and to inform operational decisions (Merriam-Webster, n.d.).

Data identity. As originally introduced in this book, data identity is a six-component combination of knowledge, skills, and abilities that enables one to make informed decisions. This book asserts that each person's data identity is comprised of a unique combination of 24 subcomponents for which one has varying levels of proficiency. In ideal scenarios, one who thoroughly understands their data identity can identify opportunities to leverage their combination of abilities to contribute to a project. A professional's data identity is influenced by several factors, including current and past work experiences, formal preparation, and work environments.

Data-informed. A type of decision-making that includes the intentional gathering, review, and use of analytics and other types of information. In some instances, data-informed is a more applicable term than data-driven, which implies that the data are deciding outcomes. In most cases, a professional uses data as a resource that provides more context to inform a decision. In essence, data do not drive.

Data literacy. The extent to which one can understand and describe quantitative or qualitative information for the purpose of addressing a challenge, monitoring progress, understanding a scenario, planning for the future, or another business-related activity.

Lagging indicators. Metrics that describe the progress of a longer term outcome. An example is a graduation rate, as students typically need a longer period of time to complete a credential than would be necessary to complete other tasks such as registering for a course or visiting a support center.

Leading indicators. Metrics that describe the progress of a shorter term outcome. Such indicators can be used to glean the extent to which a student is on track to graduate without excess hours. An example is the completion of the Federal Application for Federal Student Aid (FAFSA), as students who complete the FAFSA are likely planning to enroll or continue taking courses at the institution in pursuit of a credential.

Methods and Tools

Artificial intelligence. Computer systems that undertake tasks usually thought to require human cognitive processes and decision-making capabilities (Bowen et al., 2017). To exhibit intelligence, computers apply algorithms to find patterns in large amounts of data—a process called machine learning, which plays a key role in a number of artificial intelligence applications (Bowen et al., 2017).

Descriptive analytics. An approach that focuses on outcomes with little context and often no correlation among data points. For example, a campus could decide to conduct a survey of first-generation students to ask about their experiences with the career center. Perhaps descriptive analyses reveal that of the 1,000 students who responded to the survey, 40% said the center's resources were useful in their pursuit of a work opportunity. Additional descriptive statistics may also show that of those 40%, half had already attained a work opportunity in a prior term. While these descriptive analytics are interesting, it would be helpful for the campus to pair such results with additional analyses to gather more insight about the actual influence of the center on students' job attainment.

Machine learning. A method of designing systems that can learn, adjust, and improve based on the data included in the systems. The machine operates on continuous additions of various predictive and statistical algorithms and over time will, if the information is used effectively, provide more accurate insights to the user (Dontha, 2017).

Predictive analytics. The use of data, statistical algorithms, and machine learning techniques to identify the likelihood of future outcomes based on historical data (SAS, n.d.). The goal of predictive analytics is to go beyond knowing what has happened to providing a best assessment of what will happen in the future (SAS, n.d.). With regard to higher education, many institutions use algorithms that predict the likelihood of certain student outcomes based on historical data from at least five years or longer.

Prescriptive analytics. An approach that is focused on deriving a recommendation of what action should be taken. Prescriptive analyses are often used in combination with predictive analytics, which provide a likelihood of a certain outcome. For example, an institution may conduct a predictive analysis, the results of which suggest that transfer students who are majoring in biology will have a lower likelihood of completing a credential without excess hours. Following a review of that analysis, the campus may choose to prescribe an intervention that provides additional services and resources to support those students.

Structures and Rules

Data governance. The set of policies and procedures that a campus uses to manage data. For example, institutions that have effectively addressed data governance have clear practices for how data should be stored and accessed.

Data security. The extent to which institutions manage sensitive information. For example, data security measures often include specific guidelines regarding which individuals can access certain types of information. Data security measures can also include, but are not limited to, strategies such as routine changes of passwords for files; special storage locations for servers; and background checks for professionals who will access confidential information. Data security can also be described as the extent to which sensitive information is at risk of being accessed publicly.

Family Educational Rights and Privacy Act (FERPA). The federal law that addresses who can access a student's education records. With regard to higher education, when a student turns 18 years old or enters a postsecondary institution at any age, the rights under FERPA transfer from the parent to the student (U.S. Department of Education, n.d.-b). Institutions are responsible for managing students' educational records appropriately, including addressing who can access or modify items such as the academic transcript.

Health Insurance Portability and Accountability Act (HIPAA). The federal law that addresses health care coverage, health care fraud and abuse, industry-wide standards for health care information on electronic billing and other processes, and the protection and confidential handling of protected health information (California Department of Health Care Services, n.d.). With regard to higher education, professionals should adhere to HIPAA requirements when handling students' and professionals' health care-related data.

Institutional research. A functional area in higher education with duties that include identifying information needs; collecting, analyzing, interpreting, and reporting information; planning and evaluation; stewardship of data and information; and education of various producers, users, and consumers of information (Association for Institutional Research, n.d.-a). One might also describe institutional research as a profession, as those who perform these duties have the title of institutional researcher.

In order for campuses to achieve the widespread and positive campus climate for data use that Gagliardi and Turk (2017) described, their actions must go beyond certain offices or divisions. Such a goal requires time and consistent effort, as a variety of factors can make it difficult to create a long-term, sustainable climate for data-informed decision-making. Such factors include a tension between internal and external demands and the rapid pace at which data can be gathered and shared from multiple sources.

If a campus is attempting to balance a variety of internal and external demands, the likelihood of tension is high. This is especially relevant when multiple stakeholders want and need data for different purposes. For example, a publicly funded institution may need to gather data to report to a state system office, and such data may be equally as important to the institution's board of trustees. The advancement office of a small privately funded institution may need data regarding the rates at which recent graduates donate to the institution, and such data may also be of interest to the president of the alumni association. Data are valuable and, as a result, competing priorities may create difficulty in coordinating the gathering and use of data across offices. However, it is imperative that professionals continuously seek opportunities to align and integrate their data work with others, as doing so could reduce the formation of silo functions.

As institutions strive to provide the most accurate depiction of their progress toward various goals and outcomes, it is possible that data collection and analysis occurs rapidly and across the campus. Such a pace may seem promising for a high-functioning institution. However, without the appropriate level of planning and strategy, the climate for data use across departments and divisions can become negative, as multiple interpretations of data, differing perspectives on how to address results, and limited time to make decisions can create high levels of pressure and a less collaborative environment. Every campus professional engages in work that can impact students' progress, the delivery of programs and services, and the stewardship of resources. Therefore, it is important for everyone to approach their work with a clear plan for which data will be used and for which purposes.

This is both a challenging and promising time to work in the field of higher education. Now, arguably more than ever, college administrators, staff, faculty, and even students are surrounded by questions and debates about the extent to which a college credential will lead to desirable outcomes. As a result, many institutions are attempting to use data to dispel doubts about the value of a college experience. One challenge with such efforts is that the rapid pace of demand for data is often not aligned with the number of people who feel ready to use it to its fullest potential. It could be because of a need for more training, as Parnell et al. (2018) found that of the components typically included in an institution's data-informed strategies, training ranked the lowest.

The frequently used terms defined in this chapter are part of a common language that is often used on campuses to describe how data is managed and used. The list of terms is not exhaustive but sufficient for professionals to engage in conversations. In addition to an understanding of these terms, the foundation of one's readiness to use data is a strong understanding of what comprises their data identity. The next chapter introduces the data identity framework, a set of six core abilities that each higher education professional possesses to some extent.

THE DATA IDENTITY FRAMEWORK

Legislators are going to continue asking for more evidence of stewardship of mission attainment as justification for increasingly tight budgets. We're looking at some statistics on rising health care costs for our state and it puts pressure on the budget and we're going to have to continue making our case about what's the return for our investment in public higher education. We have to be very thoughtful and intentional about it and we have to be vigilant about capturing the right evidence to help tell our story.

—Andrew Morse, University of Northern Iowa

The previous quote (A. Morse, personal communication, March 10, 2020) describes accountability as one of the myriad priorities that exist in higher education. In order to effectively respond to countless needs for information, institutions must have groups of professionals with varying skillsets working together in a consistent and productive way. This book asserts that everyone has a data identity. While there are countless courses, certifications, reports, articles, books, and other resources to help professionals attain certain data-related skills, there appear to be few, if any, resources that comprehensively describe how these various skills fit together. This chapter addresses that need by introducing the data identity framework, a six-category combination of essential abilities that higher education professionals should possess and strive to strengthen.

The data identity framework is an adaptation of concepts from Henke et al. (2018), who state that many industries will experience a shortage of people who are skilled at data translation. They add that in order for someone to be an effective data translator, the person must be able to do three things: analyze statistics; clearly communicate complex information; and understand industry trends. Henke et al. (2018) suggest that by the year 2026, millions of data translators will be needed across industries.

While statistical prowess, communication abilities, and knowledge of industry are good capacities to have, with regard to higher education, there are additional abilities that are important as well. Thus, the data identity framework includes a total of six capacity areas to more thoroughly reflect the knowledge that higher education professionals need to contribute to and make data-informed decisions.

Interviews with professionals at varying experience levels revealed the likelihood that everyone has the capacity to use data and information to make decisions in their work. Every individual acknowledged making a data-informed decision at a frequency of at least once per week. While not every person interviewed described extensive knowledge of sophisticated methodologies, all of the professionals mentioned several additional skills that are important for everyone to have. Thus, the interviews solidified the six components of the data identity framework, which are: curiosity and inquiry; research and analysis; communication and consultation; campus context; industry context; and strategy and planning. This chapter describes the relevance of each area and establishes the foundation for chapter 7, which features a self-assessment exercise to help professionals identify the strongest areas of their data identity.

Understanding the Framework

The data identity framework is framed by the following four principles regarding individuals' abilities, the value of each component, and how the components relate to one's daily work:

1. Each component is a valuable part of one's data identity. Therefore, the components are not provided in a sequential or ranking order.
2. Every higher education professional has some level of ability in each of the areas, even if the ability is minimal. It is expected that within each component, some professionals will have much more experience and knowledge while others have less. This is especially true for the research and analysis component. This book does not assert that every professional is ready to begin work in a full-time role that is responsible for high-priority data analysis and reporting. However, this chapter is intended to describe how nearly everyone engages in some level of work related to research and analysis and the other five areas.
3. All six components are valuable to engaging in collaborative work on a campus. This presents an opportunity for colleagues to discuss how

their respective strengths can be complementary when engaging in data-informed projects together.

4. The level and frequency at which professionals engage in activities related to each component will vary. While everyone likely uses each component in their work to some extent, professionals will use certain components more or less often depending on their role and responsibilities.

As the title of this book asserts, every higher education professional, regardless of their job, is a data person. Every position on a campus, whether it is full- or part-time, executive-level, early-career, or somewhere in between, connects to data. Thus, the data identity framework is applicable to anyone who works in a higher education-related setting. As shown in Figure 2.1, the components of the framework address skills and abilities that are essential to leading or contributing to data-informed discussions, decision-making, and strategy development. Each component is described with examples of what an emerging, developing, and strong level of competence could include.

Figure 2.1. Components of the data identity framework.

Curiosity and Inquiry Ability to formulate and ask clear questions	**Research and Analysis** Ability to select and use appropriate methodologies
Communication and Consultation Ability to clearly discuss findings with multiple audiences	**Campus Context** Knowledge of current issues and trends within the institution
Industry Context Knowledge of current issues and trends in higher education	**Strategy and Planning** Ability to select and execute a course of action

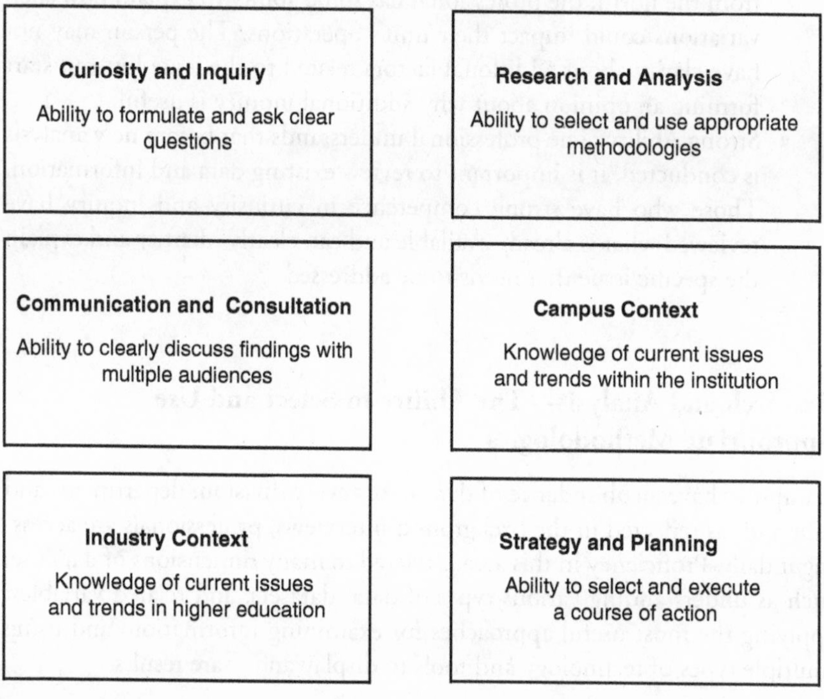

Curiosity and Inquiry—The Ability to Formulate and Ask Clear Questions

Most data-related discussions are derived from a question or issue regarding a current condition. For example, a director of a campus health and wellness center may be interested in the rates at which students visit the center during off-peak hours. The director could use the visit data to inform a broader examination of whether center staffing levels are appropriate for serving students during off-peak hours. Professionals should embrace their curiosity about the impact of their work while developing their ability to ask purposeful and practical questions for which data can be used.

Examples Related to Curiosity and Inquiry

- Emerging Ability: A professional can identify issues that need attention. In such scenarios, the professional understands patterns and can recognize details that appear to be different from the usual condition. Although the person may not have significant knowledge of how to assess the impact of the variation, their awareness of the issue is valuable.
- Developing Ability: In addition to identifying details that are different from the norm, the professional has some ability to explain how such variations could impact their unit's operations. The person may not have clarity about additional factors related to the issue but can start forming an opinion about why additional inquiry is useful.
- Strong Ability: The professional understands that before new analysis is conducted, it is important to review existing data and information. Those who have strong competence in curiosity and inquiry have reviewed what is already available and can clearly identify and explain the specific issue that needs to be addressed.

Research and Analysis—The Ability to Select and Use Appropriate Methodologies

Campuses have an abundance of data across every division, department, and unit and, as reflected in the background interviews, professionals are accessing it daily. Proficiency in this area is related to many dimensions of data use, such as understanding various types of data, datasets, and related variables; applying the most useful approaches for examining information; and using multiple types of technology and tools to display and share results.

Examples Related to Research and Analysis

- Emerging Ability: The professional understands which types of data and information are most related to their daily work. Although the person may not have a full understanding of how to connect various types of data to address an issue, the ability to identify, gather, and organize relevant data and information is useful.
- Developing Ability: In addition to understanding the majority of the various data sources available, the professional can consult with colleagues who inquire about an issue and suggest which information is needed. The professional may need assistance with advanced methodologies and analyses, but their ability to select and prepare the necessary data and conduct basic analyses is helpful.
- Strong Ability: The professional has deep understanding of historical data trends in their department. As a result, the person can determine the most useful methodology to efficiently analyze information and address an issue. This go-to person is often engaged in strategy and planning activities that leverage data to proactively use resources and address students' needs.

Communication and Consultation—The Ability to Clearly Discuss Findings With Multiple Audiences

The process of sharing data can be complex, especially when the information describes a variety of situations, synopses, and stories. Even in moments when the appropriate data and analyses are available, ineffective discussion of results can hinder a group's progress. Communication and consultation are essential to data-informed decision-making, because when everyone involved in a project discussion can understand the nuances of the work, the plan of action is clearer. This component focuses on knowing which types of information are relevant to various audiences, selecting the appropriate methods for sharing findings, and identifying when follow-up discussions are needed.

Examples Related to Communication and Consultation

- Emerging Ability: A professional can identify the information that is needed for a discussion. The person is also aware of various roles and responsibilities in their department, either from routine meetings or work experience at the campus.
- Developing Ability: In addition to selecting the most applicable information for discussions, the person can determine both the level

of detail to provide and the best method for facilitating a discussion of the information. For example, a professional with developing ability often prepares a range of summaries, including memos, reports, and other updates, and understands which type of deliverable is best for certain discussions.

- Strong Ability: The professional can explain complex findings with clarity and for a variety of audiences. Someone with strong ability is excellent at tailoring their delivery of information to colleagues' specific interests and explaining implications from multiple vantage points. This level of proficiency also involves engaging in follow-up consultations for which additional relevant data is provided.

Campus Context—Knowledge of Current Issues and Trends Within the Institution

Campus context is an essential component of one's data identity because an understanding of the institution provides the necessary perspective for a professional to conduct their work. For example, if a professional were to read a news article that highlights effective orientation programming for onboarding military-connected students, it would be helpful for the person to know which of the strategies could be feasible for their campus. Competence in this area includes varying levels of awareness of resources, programs, initiatives, and related activities within departments and across the institution.

Examples Related to Campus Context

- Emerging Ability: The professional is familiar with frequently referenced outcome measures for students at their campus. Such measures include the four- and six-year graduation rate, percentage of students from priority populations, and the highest demand fields of study at the institution. The person also understands the campus mission and most activities within their office or unit.
- Developing Ability: In addition to knowing about activities within their office, someone who is developing competence related to campus context is also aware of most activities within their division. For example, an assistant director of the student union may also know about student services work led by other units such as orientation, conduct, or health and wellness.
- Strong Ability: The person is aware of shifts in campus priorities over the previous few years. The professional is also aware of most

current campus-wide activities or initiatives, especially those related to retaining students and enhancing the educational experience. Strong ability in this area can also include knowledge of local or state contexts that impact the institution, such as internship agreements with community partners or state performance-based funding criteria.

Industry Context—Knowledge of Current Issues and Trends in Higher Education

In addition to campus context, it is important for professionals to understand the factors that influence the progression of higher education as a viable and sustainable industry. Although the field is complex, as it connects to countless external stakeholders such as governing bodies, philanthropic groups, private companies, licensing boards, communities, and other groups, professionals who commit to learning about the industry will be able to identify how well their institution is positioned to survive and thrive. This skill involves knowing how one's campus is performing and progressing in the context of other institutions, especially those that have a similar mission or size and those in the same sector of higher education.

Examples Related to Industry Context

- Emerging Ability: The professional knows the main historical and current characteristics of institutions in their sector. For example, someone who works at a community college would understand the open-access mission upon which many of the first community colleges in the United States were founded.
- Developing Ability: In addition to understanding the broad characteristics of institutions in their sector, the person can explain distinctions between their campus and other institutions of similar size, mission, and student population served. For example, a person who works at a small private college and is developing skills related to industry context might be able to describe whether the size of their incoming cohort of first-year students is larger, smaller, or similar in size to incoming cohorts at other small colleges.
- Strong Ability: Someone who is exceptionally knowledgeable of industry trends can identify the leading opportunities and challenges for approaching an issue, especially in the context of what has been successful or difficult for other campuses. Those who possess this level

of ability are often able to provide multiple case scenarios from which colleagues can learn and analyze their situation.

Strategy and Planning—The Ability to Select and Execute a Course of Action

This skill highlights the connections among all six components of the data identity framework, as a solid course of action relies on a clearly described issue, trustworthy analysis in the context of the campus and industry, and broad understanding of what is needed from all who are involved. Strategy and planning involves determining the steps needed to address an issue and developing those actions into a reasonable process and timeline.

Examples Related to Strategy and Planning

- Emerging Ability: The professional typically has a good understanding of which people should be involved in most data-related conversations. Although the person may not be as knowledgeable of each person's specific experiences and abilities, their ability to select the appropriate people and prepare a meeting agenda is helpful in planning discussions.
- Developing Ability: A professional can determine which data are valuable to discussing an issue, especially when multiple types of information are available. Those with developing ability are also adept at identifying clear roles and opportunities for each person to contribute to the discussion and related activities.
- Strong Ability: One who is highly proficient with strategy and planning is skilled at developing a step-by-step plan for efficiently using data and information to address an issue. The professional can not only prioritize activities with ease, but does so in a way that considers how results can be used in the long and short term to further the campus mission.

The data identity framework is intended to guide professionals' understanding of the many ways in which they already contribute to data-informed decision-making and spark ideas for how to increase their contributions in the future. Those who better understand their data identity may find their team engagements more fulfilling, as many roles and competencies are complementary. In fact, chapter 7 explains how multiple combinations of the six competencies can be leveraged to achieve results. The next chapter further emphasizes the importance of all competency areas and provides examples of the types of work that connect to each component. The chapter also suggests how one can build their experience in each area by seeking available resources.

3

HOW TO PROGRESS ALONG THE DATA IDENTITY CONTINUUM

One of the things I do, in addition to my actual day job, is teach the data visualization software. One of the components I've added to that curriculum, in addition to "here's how you use the software," is a focus on why you actually choose a type of chart, what sort of questions you are trying to answer, and what sort of narrative you are hoping to present. I like coaching someone through that soft skill.

—Maggie Fiock, Washington University

This quote (M. Fiock, personal communication, November 18, 2019) captures several elements that are useful when progressing along the data identity continuum. As mentioned in the previous chapter, most professionals will have a stronger ability in some areas and an emerging or developing ability in others. Two steps that will help any professional as they better understand their data identity are to maintain connections with colleagues and prioritize opportunities to learn. This chapter builds on the foundation of the newly introduced data identity framework by explaining some tangible steps that one can take to enhance their data identity. Each of the six core components is presented with a focus on example actions that one can take in their daily work. These actions cover all three levels of proficiency and highlight opportunities for engaging with a colleague and seeking low- or no-cost resources. The chapter concludes with five things that professionals should remember as they learn more about their data identity.

Step 1: Find a Data Partner

Every person interviewed for this book described a regular interaction with a colleague for the purpose of discussing data or information.

The professionals shared varying structures for the interactions, as some were one-on-one meetings and others were larger group meetings. The interviews confirmed the primary benefit of these routine engagements as the opportunity to share ideas with colleagues. For example, several professionals expressed that by talking with a colleague about various questions, they were able to identify new perspectives from which to examine issues. Professionals also described a level of increased comfort with knowing that a colleague would be willing to help with more complex projects in which data would be used to solve a problem.

Step 2: Prioritize Learning by Acquiring Low- or No-Cost Resources

Low- or no-cost resources are useful initial options for learning about relevant topics. Reports, briefs, and online trainings can expose professionals to emerging issues and prompt more substantive professional development. For example, one might decide to attend a free live briefing about a new regulation from the U.S. Department of Education. The short briefing could highlight areas where additional training would be useful and help one make a more informed choice of resources to pursue. The following are examples of activities and resources for one to consider at the emerging, developing, and strong levels of competence. References to specific resources do not indicate a formal endorsement or vetting of the material. For more information about each resource, one should follow up with the respective authors, institutions, or organizations.

Curiosity and Inquiry—The Ability to Formulate and Ask Clear Questions

Those who are skilled at developing useful questions are often good at listening to and conversing with colleagues. Their habit of engaging in discussions helps them better understand multiple perspectives, recognize patterns in details, and hone their interests around relevant topics. One who is interested in strengthening their capacity to ask clear questions should consistently think about how to not only gather and analyze data but how such data can be used for a specific purpose.

One way to gather examples of specific questions is to subscribe to a listserv and take notes about the types of topics discussed. Three things to look for while reading a listserv posting are: (a) the relevance or timeliness of the issue, (b) the specific audience that would benefit from the group's input, and (c) a description of how the responses can serve a useful purpose. For instance, the University of Kentucky College of Education maintains the ASSESS listserv, which is an opportunity for assessment professionals to share information and discuss important topics (Association for the Assessment of Learning in Higher Education, n.d.-a).

Example Activities Related to Curiosity and Inquiry

- Emerging Ability: an assistant director in the registrar's office observed an increase in the number of students who requested a copy of their transcript near the middle of the fall academic term. The assistant director compared the requests to the number of requests during the fall term of the previous year and found that over half of the requests for transcripts from both years were from students whose major was biology. The assistant director then emailed a short summary of the details to colleagues in the office and requested a meeting to discuss next steps.
- Developing Ability: a director of student activities noticed that more students registered for programs that were announced via email than those that were announced via social media. The director gathered additional information to compare event registration rates on days in which announcements were made via email or social media. The director also reviewed the results of a prior year survey of students regarding their interest in participating in new campus activities. The director then scheduled a meeting with colleagues to discuss how the office could better leverage communications to increase students' engagement.
- Strong Ability: an associate vice president (AVP) for alumni giving is leading a campus work group that is focused on increasing the giving rates of those who graduated from the institution within the past five years. The AVP reviewed the prior five years of giving information and determined that the group should focus on graduates who, based on the most recent contact information, live within a 250-mile radius of the campus. The AVP then developed a set of specific questions for the group to address as they developed a giving campaign.

Free Resource

Yeado et al. (2014) released a brief that is a practical guide for higher education professionals to ask thought-provoking questions. The title of the brief includes the exact words "analyses to provoke discussion and action."

The document contains 10 well-explained scenarios that professionals at any level can use as examples for how to frame clear questions.

Research and Analysis—The Ability to Select and Use Appropriate Methodologies

One frequently asked question among higher education professionals is related to the selection of software. It is common for one to be curious about the technology that is best suited for analytics work, and while it is a relevant question, it is arguably not the most critical one. The more important priority is for professionals to have a solid understanding of how the software can support the method by which data will be used. For example, when someone learns to drive a vehicle, the preparation materials are not focused on the selection of a specific vehicle but instead on how the automobile should be used to get from one place to another. A driver's education course does not recommend a certain vehicle but instead is designed to show the learner how to complete certain maneuvers, understand road signs, and select the appropriate speed. Just as a person learning to drive is more focused on how an automobile should be used, higher education professionals who desire to increase their research and analysis skills should prioritize understanding various methods, as that is essential to making data-informed decisions with fidelity.

Example Activities Related to Research and Analysis

- Emerging Ability: a campus general counsel asks the assistant director of compliance to provide a three-year report of any areas in which the campus has had violations of the Jeanne Clery Disclosure of Campus Security Policy and Campus Crime Statistics Act, also referred to as the Clery Act. The assistant director gathers a list of all violations for the period, sorts the list by number of violations, develops categories for the violations, and shares the results.
- Developing Ability: a faculty member who notices a decline in students' engagement with the institution's learning management system wants to gather feedback from students about their preferred method of communication. The faculty member talks with a colleague who has noticed a similar pattern and together they develop a short survey and student focus group questions. They then invite other faculty in the department to provide input.
- Strong Ability: a data analyst in the school of arts and sciences conducts a five-year study of transfer students' progress in calculus courses.

The goal of the study is to identify factors that appear to influence the rates at which transfer students complete calculus courses on the first attempt.

Free Resource

The Association for Institutional Research (n.d.-b) has a group page on LinkedIn. The page provides a space for professionals to share questions, news articles, and resources. The page is not exclusive to those who are working in an institutional research office, but it does require viewers to have a free LinkedIn account.

Communication and Consultation—The Ability to Clearly Discuss Findings With Multiple Audiences

As mentioned in chapter 2, proficiency in communication and consultation relies upon one understanding how to deliver information in multiple ways for colleagues who have varying roles. The goal of this component is not to perfect the use of a specific method such as a dashboard, memorandum, or long-form report, but instead to know when certain approaches are most helpful in particular settings. Each type of communication is valuable and those who are skilled communicators and consultants can routinely determine which option is best.

Example Activities Related to Communication and Consultation

- Emerging Ability: the chief of staff to a campus president is responsible for preparing the agenda for each cabinet meeting. Prior to the meetings, the chief of staff gathers discussion topics from the president and cabinet members, finds common themes among the list of priorities, and prepares the agenda accordingly for each item.
- Developing Ability: a director of the health and wellness center wants to encourage all members of the campus community to proactively address their mental health. The director forms a workgroup comprised of faculty, staff, and students to develop methods for promoting the available campus programs and services. The workgroup develops infographics about mental health among college professionals and students and messages about healthy behaviors that are tailored for each audience.
- Strong Ability: a director of information technology is responsible for helping the office of financial aid discontinue using an older

technology platform and start using a newly deployed one. Prior to the launch of the new system, the director researched the primary functions of the financial aid office. Rather than simply provide a copy of the user manual or links to online training videos, the director prepared a memo that described how each financial aid professional's primary job duties in the old platform could be performed in the new system. The director customized the memos to translate the exact responsibilities in the context of the new system. After the launch of the new system, the director scheduled office hours to provide additional consultation and support.

Who has this time to write or read

Free Resource

The Education Trust website College Results Online is a useful resource for professionals who are interested in demographic information about four-year institutions in the United States. The publicly available website has features that allow visitors to compare graduation rates for multiple institutions at once. The website is a good example of how to present information that can be consumed by multiple audiences, as the home page describes College Results Online as a resource designed to provide information to policymakers, counselors, parents, and students (The Education Trust, n.d.).

Campus Context—Knowledge of Current Issues and Trends Within the Institution

Those who intend to strengthen their campus context can start by learning as much as possible about routine activities in their office, department, and the institution. A good first step in the process is to select a primary office activity and review its progress and evolution for the last three years. Gathering historical context highlights shifts in office priorities, which provides a foundation for asking clear and relevant questions.

Example Activities Related to Campus Context

- Emerging Ability: an assistant professor who teaches in a master's in public administration program is interested in revising the department's new student orientation program. The professor reviews survey results from prior orientation attendees and gathers data on the rates at which students who attend orientation complete the program without excess hours. The professor also consults with faculty in other academic departments to learn about their orientation strategies and gather input on how changes to orientation programming could impact the overall student experience.

- Developing Ability: a group of colleagues in the division of student affairs partner to develop a learning event in which each office shares a set of current initiatives. For example, in 2017, the University at Albany's division of student affairs held "Dane-X," a division-wide learning event in which each department presented their current work and how it contributed to the mission of the institution. In 2018, the University of Tennessee hosted an assessment symposium in which assessment professionals from across the institution gathered to learn about each other's work and share suggestions for future collaboration.

- Strong Ability: an assistant director in the office of undergraduate research serves on a committee focused on examining how the institution's learning outcomes are embedded in multiple campus opportunities. The assistant director is knowledgeable of a variety of activities throughout the institution, including on-campus student employment, internship programs, assistantships, cocurricular programs, experiential learning courses, and other types of engagements for which evidence of students' learning is available.

Free Resource

Fresno State University (n.d.) has a student cupboard, which provides food and hygiene resources to students in need. For those who are interested in the rates at which students are visiting the cupboard, the university has a publicly available web page that provides trend data by semester and month. The resource is a good example of how campus professionals can gain a quick perspective of the extent to which students may be experiencing financial hardship.

Industry Context—Knowledge of Current Issues and Trends in Higher Education

A periodic review of how one's institution compares and differs from other campuses in the United States can reveal opportunities for improvement and indicators of progress. The goal of gaining industry context is not to identify a list of best practices by which one's own work should be measured but instead to understand how campuses of similar size and sector are approaching common issues. The following quote from Laura Wankel at Northeastern

University (personal communication, October 24, 2019) explains this concept well:

> We have a fact book like most campuses do and I trust the information that our institutional research office puts out, our own enrollment data, and the national surveys we might participate in like CIRP or NSSE. So, depending on where that information may be held, I've generally used all of that in all of my roles. I think it informs program design and response and understanding the student culture. So, I think there's value in some of those national things and I do use them.

Example Activities Related to Industry Context

- Emerging Ability: a director of adult and continuing education at a regional comprehensive institution attends a virtual training event in which national experts describe current trends related to career and technical education in rural environments. The training event includes a set of case studies that the director reviews to learn how other campuses are providing services.
- Developing Ability: an assistant director of institutional research at a community college invites institutional research professionals from other community colleges in the area to join a monthly video call. The meetings provide a space for professionals to network and share strategies for addressing common issues such as rates of persistence and prerequisite course completion.
- Strong Ability: the vice president of academic affairs is preparing to deliver a presentation to the campus board of trustees regarding the rates at which priority populations graduate from the institution's nursing department in comparison to other institutions. The vice president hosts focus groups with nursing faculty and students, reviews national benchmarking reports, and consults national organizations. The presentation addresses the graduation rates of nursing students who are from low-income backgrounds, are first-generation college goers, and have underrepresented or previously marginalized identities. The presentation compares the total enrollment, cost, and licensure pass rates for the program to those of other institutions.

Free Resource

The American Association of Community Colleges (AACC) produces fact sheets that provide easy-to-understand graphics and figures to describe current trends in the community college sector. The short documents typically address topics such as the percentage of community college students who receive federal financial aid, headcount enrollment, and demographic attributes of students enrolled for credit (AACC, 2020).

Strategy and Planning—The Ability to Select and Execute a Course of Action

The two steps mentioned in the start of this chapter are especially relevant to strategy and planning, as collaboration with colleagues and continuous learning can propel a project from the conceptual phase to the action phase. Those who strive to build their capacity in this area often engage in activities that address the intersection of people, processes, and priorities. The following quote from Michael Baston at Rockland Community College (personal communication, October 31, 2019) is an example of how a professional can create a balanced approach for using data to make decisions:

> There are four specific types of data that I look at. I look at data for purposes of planning because if I'm going to allocate resources, I need to understand the implications of using one set of resources to address another set of issues. So, I use it for purposes of planning. I use it for purposes of continuous improvement because if you're not able to have a sense of your baseline realities, then you can't know if interventions that you're going to put in place can possibly make a difference. The third thing is predictions. It's the predictive nature of assessment, for example, and enrollment. I have to look at past patterns and pain points so I can determine effectively how to predict what could come based on our information. And then lastly, I use data for celebration because you have to be able to identify ways in which you're making a positive impact and highlight those, lift those up, and celebrate.

Example Activities Related to Strategy and Planning

- Emerging Ability: the assistant coach of the women's track and field team is preparing a draft travel budget for the next season. The goal is to identify savings of 20% without compromising the students' academic commitments or lessening the quality of the travel experience. The assistant coach reviews the travel expenses from the prior season, consults with the athletic department about any existing partnerships that include discount pricing, and talks with the team to gather their input about the parts of the travel experience that are most and least enjoyable and helpful. The assistant coach then develops a summary of findings and shares with the other members of the coaching staff.

- Developing Ability: the assistant controller is responsible for identifying options for how the office can reduce the number of paper checks that are disbursed. The assistant controller invites colleagues to engage in a process mapping exercise that shows the specific actions that must occur from the point when a payment is requested to when a check is created. Following the exercise, the assistant controller works with colleagues to research how other organizations of a similar size are managing their accounts payable processes. The group reconvenes to discuss which parts of the process can be managed more efficiently with technology, and the assistant director prepares a proposal of options for the controller's review.
- Strong Ability: the director of fraternity and sorority life (FSL) is developing a summer training for the advisers to each Greek letter organization. The campus president is interested in the extent to which students' participation in fraternity or sorority life positively impacts their preparation for employment, graduate study, and other post-graduation options. The director designs the training to address the president's inquiry by inviting a group of recent graduates to share their experiences and a group of local employers and graduate admissions officers to share perspectives. The training also includes a set of workshops that focus on how to identify and assess learning in cocurricular settings. The training concludes with the director sharing a plan for the metrics that the advisers should monitor each month. Following the training, the director schedules quarterly discussions with the advisers to discuss their progress with data monitoring and offer any needed support.

Free Resource

Burnside et al. (2019) conducted a national landscape analysis of institutions' delivery of on-campus student employment programs. As a follow up to the research, NASPA–Student Affairs Administrators in Higher Education (2019) released a self-assessment rubric to guide institutions through the process of evaluating their on-campus student employment program. The rubric covers six areas that, if institutions address effectively with strategy and planning, will result in students having a high-quality on-campus employment experience. The comprehensive nature of the self-assessment, especially the explanations of the rating categories, is a good example of how to strategically design a program and use resources appropriately.

The following quote from Tim Bono at Washington University in St. Louis (personal communication, October 23, 2019) highlights the main premise of this book, which is that everyone is using data and information. Although each professional has a different approach for deciphering which information should be used and when, there are five rules that everyone should consider when owning their data identity. These rules, if adopted by everyone on a campus, can help professionals use data thoroughly and thoughtfully. The five rules are related to data literacy, managing complex change, timing of decisions, considerate uses of data, and clarity of goals.

> I am trained as a behavioral scientist. That is my background. And virtually all of our understanding of human behavior, how we interact with each other, and how we make decisions is based on data. Sometimes people assume that using data has to involve some sophisticated regression analysis or hierarchical multinomial modeling. And certainly data in that form can inform decisions. But data encompasses so much more than that. I think about data as synonymous with information, whether that is things like numerical information that you calculate on an Excel sheet or just data about your own intuition.
>
> For example, I went to a restaurant last night that I really liked. So I will use that data—that I really liked the place—to recommend it to others and to return there again myself. Data sets like that are not necessarily numbers that I've written down or calculated, but nonetheless, they are pieces of information that will influence decisions I make in the future. I am constantly using data, both formally and informally. It's part and parcel of who I am, how I do things, and how I make decisions.

Rule 1: Strive to Be Data Literate

As mentioned in this book's introduction, Swing and Ross (2016) predicted that in the future, a wider range of staff will be users and consumers of data. This creates a great need for a culture that promotes and encourages higher education professionals to increase their data literacy. Chapter 1 defines data literacy as the extent to which one can understand and describe quantitative or qualitative information for the purpose of addressing a challenge, monitoring progress, understanding a scenario, planning for the future, or another business-related activity. Similar to other skills and abilities for which more experience can improve one's competence, increasing one's data literacy should be an ongoing professional development goal.

Rule 2: Everyone Is a Decision Maker

Gagliardi (2018) states that within institutions, the desire has increased among senior leaders, administrators, faculty, advisers, and staff to use decision analytics to benefit students and ensure that the institution continues to grow. Gagliardi adds that these stakeholders see the potential for transformational change, which is especially timely as more institutions strive to use their personnel, financial, and other resources to deliver high-quality student experiences. Transformational change is a complex endeavor, and Conejo (2011) suggests that organizations need five things in order to manage that complexity. Those five things are vision, skills, incentives, resources, and an action plan. Conejo (2011) also posits that depending on which of those elements is missing, organizations will experience a different type of ineffectiveness. For example, when a vision is missing, confusion can persist and when an action plan is missing, false starts might occur (Conejo, 2011).

Both Gagliardi and Conejo offer perspectives that suggest decision-making in today's higher education climate is arguably more difficult than ever. Therefore, it is a good time to introduce a new profile of a campus decision maker and affirm it as one that includes everyone, especially students. The following quote from Patrick Biddix at the University of Tennessee, Knoxville (personal communication, November 25, 2019) underscores the value of consistent connections to students:

> Some of the best data you'll ever gather is from conversations with students. A constant source of data for me is conversations with our students. Just casual and informal about how their day is going, what their classes are, and what we can do to make things better.

This second data rule asserts that everyone is responsible for a portion of campus resources. Although the portions may not be evenly distributed, each individual effort to make the best decisions possible will help ensure that quality is uncompromised and students are prioritized.

Rule 3: Do Not Rush

The pace of the campus environment is often fast, as the volume of activities is high, the number of days to provide services, programs, and instruction is limited, and the number of decisions needed is steadily increasing. These factors could lead some professionals to conclude that a faster-paced approach for analysis is best, as time-sensitive issues sometimes require more immediate actions. While a faster approach is unavoidable in certain scenarios, the majority of decisions, especially those not of an emergency nature, can be made with a slower approach. There is certainly an extent to which taking additional time can lead to indecisiveness and the often-used term "analysis paralysis," which describes one's inability to make a decision. But, for most routine business-related discussions, professionals can achieve a balance of interpreting the necessary information and doing so in a reasonable time frame. The following case scenario displays an approach for determining whether enough data have been gathered and interpreted to make a decision.

Case Scenario

A campus office of career services is redesigning its fourth annual spring employer expo event. The event, which will occur in nine months, will feature 100 organizations that are recruiting college students for internship and career positions. A team of five professionals are meeting biweekly to determine three critical planning elements: (a) the process for selecting the companies to participate, (b) the feasibility of a new process to pair students with potential employers, and (c) indicators and measures of a successful event.

Prior to their first meeting, the group addressed the following questions:

- What information is available regarding prior employers' and students' satisfaction with the event?
- What data, if any, are available regarding the extent to which students who were offered a position with a participating company are still employed with the company?
- Which companies are engaged with the campus in ways other than the annual expo?

During their subsequent meetings over the next three months, the group addressed the following questions:

- What types of existing data can be gathered to align employers' needs and students' interests? For example, for the employers that did not recruit a student following the expo, what types of positions were advertised?
- How many separate and individual communications can the team deliver to each company regarding pre-expo, expo, and post-expo opportunities?
- Which departments at the institution have high numbers of students who visit the career center?
- Which planning and performance metrics from the upcoming expo can be used for the event in future years?

By addressing these questions, the group was prepared to use the six months remaining before the event to execute a plan with reasonable allocations of time and resources. The professionals committed to delivering a thoughtful, thorough, collaborative, and data-informed experience. This case example emphasizes the third data rule, which is to avoid making rushed decisions as much as possible. More often than not, professionals who invest the appropriate amount of time will complete work more efficiently.

Rule 4: Know as Much as Possible About Students but Do Not Be Creepy

Palmer and Ekowo (2016) state that institutions use predictive analytics for three primary reasons: to identify students most in need of advising services; to develop adaptive learning courseware that personalizes learning; and to manage enrollment. As one considers the financial, time, and personnel investments that campuses make for these three things, it is no surprise that many senior leaders want to make sure that those investments return optimal results. However, as the use of predictive modeling becomes more commonplace, it is important for professionals to understand the implications of using such tools to influence students' behaviors.

Gardner (2019) states that examining data about students in aggregate format could obscure the fact that each student has a different situation and thus different needs. With regard to using data to profile students, Lane (2018) adds that the ability to track and predict student behavior has both positive and negative implications. This fourth data rule is critical, as professionals should be careful to use data in ways that illuminate solutions while not imposing on students' privacy. Federal regulations such as FERPA and HIPAA address the safeguarding of students' confidential information, but campus professionals should also remain cognizant of the more interpersonal uses of students' data and maintain appropriate boundaries.

Rule 5: Make Data Goals Clear for Everyone, Including Students

When an institution reveals its strategic priorities, it is an opportunity for the entire campus to find a connection to the vision. Students are at the center of that vision, and McNair et al. (2016) assert that when institutions are focused on helping students succeed, professionals should examine the extent to which the campus is ready for students, rather than the level at which students are ready for college. As the strategy and planning component of the data identity framework describes, selecting a course of action requires purposeful use of communication. For example, a campus that has reached a goal of increasing its graduation rate would benefit from not only displaying the news for everyone to see but also sharing the specific actions that professionals and students have taken to contribute to the outcome.

When an institution's overall goals or processes are unclear, the likelihood is high that students will not be served well. For example, Burd et al. (2018) researched how institutions use financial aid award letters to inform students about the amounts and types of aid they can expect to receive upon enrolling. The qualitative study, which included an examination of over 500 award letters to students from unique campuses, revealed several themes that describe challenges some students face when trying to interpret information provided by their institution. The research found several instances of such things as confusing jargon and terminology, omission of the complete cost to attend, and no differentiation among types of aid (Burd et al., 2018). As the cost to attend college remains expensive for some students, professionals should remember this last data rule, as it is important to make the campus mission, goals, and related activities as clear as possible.

Conclusion

This chapter focused on the many ways in which professionals can actively strengthen the parts of their data identity. These activities appear to be attainable, as the professionals who were interviewed described uses of information that included budget details, routine activity information, and data from their institution's various other systems. The interviews not only revealed the depth and breadth of professionals' access and use of data, but the myriad opportunities to interpret and discuss results. While a widespread use of data to make decisions is certainly an ultimate goal, it is important for professionals to be aware of missteps to avoid.

The five data rules presented in this chapter signal the importance of the relational aspects of managing one's data identity. As mentioned in the previous chapter, professionals can be most successful when working with data in environments that promote open communication, supportive sharing of progress and results, and ongoing collaboration. By owning the responsibility for becoming data literate, welcoming every colleague to discussions as a type of decision maker, taking the appropriate amount of time to gather and interpret information, and remembering students' perspectives, one can ensure that these rules are commonplace on campus at every level.

The challenge for many institutions that desire to increase their use of data to make decisions does not relate to a scarcity of information, as most campuses have an abundance of data. The difficulty is often more connected to selecting the focus areas for which the decisions should be made. While outcomes are a visible indicator of progress, professionals should also remember to use data to make decisions regarding needs and processes. The next chapter will explain the connections between needs, processes, and outcomes and provide examples of how one can use data to address each.

4

BACK TO BASICS: UNDERSTANDING THE BALANCE OF NEEDS, PROCESSES, AND OUTCOMES

We have enhanced our counseling staff. Based on the data that we received from our American College Health Association survey, our student needs assessment surveys, and from students being able to schedule appointments, we found that we needed to increase the number of counselors that we have on staff. So, we used that information to leverage data to then be able to garner further resources to hire more counselors.

—Patricia Martinez, University of Alabama at Birmingham

Much of the discussion in the book thus far has addressed how professionals can use data to address certain outcomes. While outcomes are often the primary focus of most public-facing reports, professionals who are intentional about also using data to examine and address needs and processes will have a broader perspective from which to make decisions. The previous quote (P. Martinez, personal communication, November 18, 2019) highlights how professionals can use data to not just improve outcomes but also to identify needs and improve processes. For the purposes of this chapter, needs, processes, and outcomes are defined as the following:

- Needs are gaps between current and desired programs, resources, or services. For example, many institutions design offerings for students who, at the time of first enrollment in college, were from low-income backgrounds. In order to deploy resources effectively, it is important for professionals to understand the varying needs these students

35

may have, such as access to a laptop or affordable transportation to campus. Professionals who are using data to identify gaps should ask questions that focus on what the needs are.

- Processes are how programs, resources, policies, or services are delivered for the purpose of improving efficiency or effectiveness. Examinations of processes often address the extent to which a practice is resulting in an optimal use of personnel or financial resources. For example, a college dean might be interested in measuring the impact of a virtual interview process for prospective students rather than an in-person experience.

- Outcomes are the results of a program, resource, policy, or service. Common outcomes that higher education professionals examine include the rates at which students persist, complete a credential, and acquire job opportunities.

The intersection of needs, processes, and outcomes can be described in multiple ways. Three such approaches are linear flow, hierarchical flow, and cyclical flow, each of which is described with the following figures.

Figure 4.1 proposes that examinations of needs, processes, and outcomes follow an order in which data could be first used to identify core needs, then to determine how current processes are addressing those needs. After one uses data to identify needs and assess impact of processes, processes can be adjusted and outcomes measured. This linear flow assumes that the issue to be corrected is heavily related to process, as it is the piece that

Figure 4.1. Linear intersection of needs, processes, and outcomes.

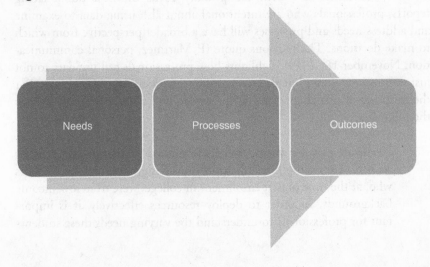

precedes the outcome. A potential limitation of this description is that it has a one-direction flow. Professionals who are more comfortable starting data discussions by focusing on desired outcomes could consider a cyclical flow, which is described later, as a better contextual frame.

As shown in Figure 4.2, the intersection of needs, processes, and outcomes can also be described as hierarchical. This type of frame, similar to a linear one, assumes that progress toward outcomes rests on effective interpretation of needs first and then processes. However, the hierarchical frame is different in that it visually does not place the same level of emphasis on each component. An analogy that explains the connection with this frame is one that relates to caring for a plant. One who is successful in caring for a plant will see a visible outcome of green leaves. However, in order to reach that outcome, one must first pay careful attention to the needs of the plant, which include positioning it in the appropriate pot, providing the required amount of soil and fertilizer, and positioning it in the correct amount of direct sunlight. One must then adhere to the appropriate processes for caring

Figure 4.2. Hierarchical intersection of needs, processes, and outcomes.

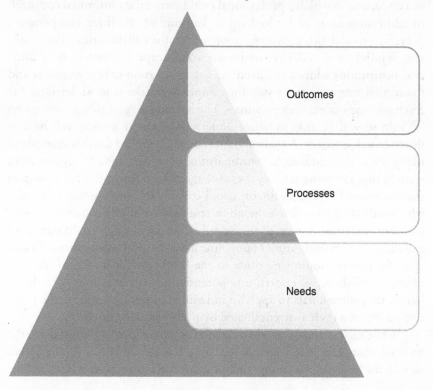

for the plant, which include routinely providing the right amount of water and pruning. After the needs and processes have been addressed, the outcomes should be visible over time.

This hierarchical analogy could apply to addressing an issue on campus. For example, a professional who is responsible for services to support part-time students might examine data related to a program and find that participation is lower than expected levels. Rather than decide that the outcome, low participation, is related to the program's value, the professional could review the analysis of needs, which should have informed the program's design. If the program, as offered, still addresses part-time students' core needs, the next step would be to review data regarding how the program is delivered. Such a review could uncover procedural aspects that led to the outcome, such as offering the program on off-peak days for class attendance or during off-peak hours in which the students are not on campus. While the hierarchical model is an effective frame for professionals who are most comfortable using data to discover areas of need, one limitation of the frame is that when not used with a schedule, it could result in professionals not allotting enough time to address processes and outcomes.

Figure 4.3 describes the intersection of needs, processes, and outcomes as a cycle, one in which a professional could start a data-informed approach to addressing an issue by looking at any one of the three components. A cyclical model also provides opportunities for collaboration. For example, Whitley et al. (2018) conducted a landscape analysis of how four-year institutions address the needs of first-generation college students and found that one important step for campuses to take is to understand the reach and gaps of existing resources. The authors suggest that practitioners who do so will be able to better understand gaps in service and use evidence-based practices. A cyclical frame could be applied for this example in many ways. For instance, a coordinator of an institution's first-generation student programming is likely aware of several services and other resources that are offered. The coordinator could collaborate with a group of faculty who routinely advise first-generation students on their academic options and thus understand some of their needs. The partnership could start with a discussion of existing student outcome measures and a discussion of strategies for jointly monitoring those in the future. While a cyclical frame is ideal for collaborative efforts, one potential limitation is that it could be harder for professionals to apply in individual project settings, as the iterative nature of a cycle is strengthened by multiple perspectives.

While each of these frames has related opportunities and limitations, the most relevant part of each figure is that the pieces are connected. Professionals should try to avoid examining one of these three components without the

Figure 4.3. Cyclical intersection of needs, processes, and outcomes.

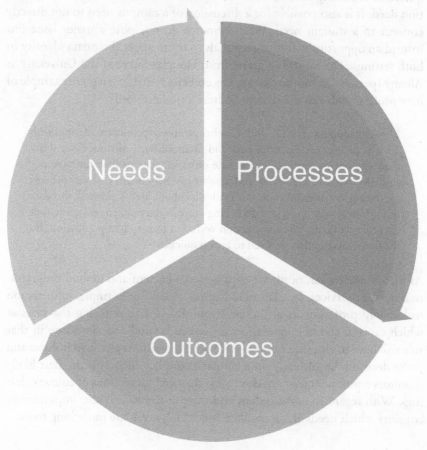

context of the other two, as it could result in an incomplete summary of issues and contribute to insufficient decisions. The remainder of this chapter provides some tangible examples of how data can be used to examine needs, processes, and outcomes.

Using Data to Examine Needs

As professionals strive to enhance their data identity, it will be helpful to apply the six components to examinations of both student needs and campus needs. For example, a vice provost who is adept at asking clear questions about students' academic needs might also ask questions regarding ongoing professional development needs for staff. It is likely that in some instances, questions regarding students' needs may not connect to an obvious institution need. It is also possible for a discussion of a campus need to not directly connect to a student need. Both scenarios do not pose a major issue but instead an opportunity for professionals to try to apply their data identity in both settings. The following quote from Douglas Sweet at the University at Albany (personal communication, December 13, 2019) is a good example of how professionals can use data to address a student need:

> I hope that on our campus and on other campuses people are sharing, with a lot of protection, financial data and financial need of students. I think that we need to continue to increase our awareness of how unstable our students might be financially and how we can help them. Our vice provost for undergraduate education and I talk a lot about how we have all this data but we always use it too late. So having more in the moment or on the spot data that we could take some action with. For our student population, it's the financial data that we need to act on quicker.

As mentioned earlier, needs are gaps between current and desired programs, resources, or services. In relation to campus needs, for example, information technology professionals are often responsible for monitoring the rates at which campus technology platforms need to be updated. Someone in that role will have to examine campus-wide need for various platform licenses and make decisions accordingly. In a similar example, a department chair likely monitors enrollment levels to determine the need for sections of course offerings. With regard to both student and campus needs, it is also important to consider which needs are immediate and which needs are more long term.

Using Data to Examine Processes

When one examines processes, the intentional emphasis on efficiency and effectiveness also reveals the importance of strategic communication. As most programs and services are not delivered with solo efforts, analyses of the process by which resources are offered must be handled with care. The overall goal when examining processes is to identify opportunities for improvement, which should be a shared effort, and the following quote from Franz Reneau at the Georgia Institute of Technology (personal communication, December 19, 2019) is a good example:

> One of the things that I'm most proud of is an opportunity for us in the office of academic effectiveness to work strategically to strengthen the

assessment process across our colleges and schools. I did a comprehensive deep dive and looked at past assessment reports that were submitted by all 148 degree programs. I studied the feedback that was provided by our institutional accrediting body.

I also spoke to key stakeholders within all of our colleges and schools to get a feel for where pain points were and narrow what we needed to do in terms of strategies to address the opportunities that I identified. So, I laid out a framework for the work that needed to happen, vetted that with the person that I reported to, and it rolled up to the provost and got the green light.

What I did was develop a framework that would help the lay person understand how what they do in their space not only impacts what students know and are able to do but how it moves the agenda for the institution in terms of our mission. I developed an approach that captured the key elements in the assessment process that were important in telling that story. I find that when folks understand the way we tell a story in a space we operate, it makes that process a lot easier.

I did a lot of training and engagement across all of our colleges and schools. Our first cycle of assessment reports were submitted this year. What I observed in terms of the quality of those reports and how programs are telling the story around student learning and student success in those degree programs was significantly different from how they did it in the past.

As professionals work together to examine processes, it is important to keep a log of major decisions that impact operations. Keeping a record that includes the date of the decision, persons involved, and the reason for the decision will provide historical context for future decisions and help professionals who are involved in related discussions in the future. Every campus will at some point experience shifts in workforce and operating budgets. Thus, professionals who record their decisions and related details will help the institution make the best use of its resources.

→ hon example - UAS change

Using Data to Examine Outcomes

Lane (2018) describes five types of data that are available to policymakers: descriptive, diagnostic, real-time, predictive, and prescriptive. Table 4.1 lists the actions and key questions that are often connected to each type of data. As one pursues using data to examine outcomes, these questions can help frame the issues. The following are Table 4.1 and a quote from Marc Harding at the University of Pittsburgh (personal communication, January 8, 2020),

TABLE 4.1
Types of Data Available to Policymakers

Type of Analysis	Descriptive	Diagnostic	Real-Time	Predictive	Prescriptive
Action	Reporting	Analysis	Monitoring	Forecasting	Impact
Key Question	What happened?	Why did it happen?	What is happening?	What will happen?	What should be done?

Source: Adaptation of Figure 11.1 from Lane (2018).

which illuminate the volume of outcomes-related data that institutions collect and analyze.

> I'm in what some in higher education would call a scoreboard unit. I'm vice provost for enrollment and much like an athletic coach or an athletics director, which would be another scoreboard unit. So would advancement or fundraising be a scoreboard unit. So would research as a scoreboard unit. By that, I mean the metrics, the key performance indicators, by which I am held responsible for and held accountable for are very public.
>
> How many students do we enroll? How many in-state students? How many out-of-state students? How many students of color? How many Pell Grant recipients? How much did we spend? There's a whole piece of what I do that is massively data-oriented.

One thing to note with regard to examining outcomes is the distinction between correlation and causation. In essence, this is related to the types of conclusions that can and should be drawn based on the results of analyses. For instance, if a professional has data showing that students who live on campus also achieve higher course grades in algebra, that does not necessarily mean that living on campus is the cause of students' better performance. The fact that students live on campus may be related to their performance, but it would not be reasonable to conclude a direct impact without more analysis. This is especially relevant to predictive and prescriptive analyses.

Conclusion

Morse and Woods (2019) state that relying on singular data points, including value-added gains, and indicators of use and satisfaction creates blind spots for educators to ensure high-quality experiences for students. The authors add that though these assessments yield important indicators of the student experience, they do not provide detailed evidence on the effectiveness of activity-level learning interventions designed to introduce or reinforce competencies expected of students (Morse & Woods, 2019). This chapter supported those assertions by describing the value of a holistic data approach, one that addresses needs, processes, and outcomes. The intersection of these concepts is a foundational frame that professionals can apply to nearly any data discussion. The next chapter continues the focus on needs, processes, and outcomes with 10 practical examples of how professionals can use data to improve the delivery of programs and services.

DATA IN ACTION PART 1: 10 WAYS TO USE DATA TO IMPROVE PROGRAMS AND SERVICES

After I do midterm evaluations, I get students' feedback. I put that up on the screen and a lot of times someone will say "I need you to lecture more" or another person says "I need more of the small group activities." So, I'll put the students' results up and communicate how I will make adjustments.

—Ann Gansemer-Topf, Iowa State University

Campuses are responsible for both creating resources to support students and ensuring that those resources are delivered at the best levels possible. The previous quote (A. Gansemer-Topf, personal communication, January 14, 2020) is a good example and supports national trends, as Parnell et al. (2018) examined the use of analytics among student affairs, information technology, and institutional research professionals and found that 71% of institutions conduct data projects with a goal of more efficient delivery of programs and services. Whether it is academic affairs professionals expanding course offerings for online learners or student affairs professionals making support services more integrated and holistic, everyone on a campus is involved in efforts to help students succeed.

For example, it is now commonplace for student retention committees to use data that range from leading and lagging indicators such as those mentioned in chapter 1 to real-time data such as assignment grades. Public–private partnerships that involve campuses working with consulting firms to predict housing costs and future enrollment are also common. As a result, the emphasis on using data to monitor and improve the quality of programs and services is part of everyone's work. The good news, which interviews confirmed, is that professionals across a campus are finding ways to leverage data to improve students' experiences. When asked to describe how their use of data resulted in something positive, several professionals explained how their approaches led to improved programs or services.

For the purpose of this chapter, a resource is considered to be a dedicated program, initiative, tool, or offering that is designed for the purpose of addressing students' academic, financial, social, or health needs. The following 10 practice examples are based on research and conversations with professionals and will address three primary areas: (a) relevance of an action to students' overall campus experience; (b) suggestions for how one can apply parts of the data identity framework; and (c) the related needs, processes, and outcomes that can be addressed by each action. Some examples will also feature an actual campus scenario, one in which a professional who was interviewed described a real instance in which data was used to improve a resource.

As a refresher, the six components of the data identity framework are provided as follows:

- Curiosity and Inquiry – the ability to formulate and ask clear questions
- Research and Analysis – the ability to select and use appropriate methodologies
- Communication and Consultation – the ability to clearly discuss findings with multiple audiences
- Campus Context – knowledge of current issues and trends within the institution
- Industry Context – knowledge of current issues and trends in higher education
- Strategy and Planning – the ability to select and execute a course of action

Example 1: Using Data to Improve Students' Access to Self-Service Resources

Students who attend institutions with physical campuses have access to several resources to support their overall health and well-being. Health and fitness centers provide learning resources and connections to other students and professionals, which can be very valuable. For example, Vasold et al. (2019) state that students who participate in a greater number of campus recreation activities and with a higher time investment are more likely to report greater benefits to physical health, psychosocial health, and learning outcomes.

As institutions strive to maximize facility use by aligning hours of operation with demand, professionals who can use data to that end will have a better chance of improving students' access to the resources they need. For instance, a campus librarian could use data regarding the rates at which students reserve study spaces in the library to develop procedures for how those shared spaces can be used. The following practice example focuses on how an assistant director of academic affairs can examine students' engagement with the tutoring center. The specific action is related to examining the process by which a student is paired with a math tutor.

In this example, the assistant director could leverage the Communication and Consulting and Strategy and Planning parts of their data identity. A good initial step would be to gather current tutors' perceptions of how their tutoring assignments match their skills and preparation for the role. Following that step, the assistant director could ask a group of students who are currently receiving tutoring services about whether the tutoring experience has helped them keep pace with their course assignments. This qualitative approach will result in feedback that the assistant director can use to engage in Strategy and Planning. The professional should note common challenges regarding scheduling, content knowledge, performance expectations, and other issues. The assistant director should also note positive aspects of the experience, such as instances when students described their level of comfort with asking for additional explanation of material.

Addressing Relevant Needs, Processes, and Outcomes

This scenario provides an example of how a professional can use data to assess how a service is meeting desired objectives. The goal is not to use data to exclusively find missteps or inefficiencies, but instead to determine if the current operation is effective or could be improved. The following are example questions that a professional who is examining a service similar to this one should consider. The questions address needs, processes, and outcomes, any one of which could impact the pairing of a student with a resource.

Needs-Related Questions

- Does the tutoring center have enough tutors to meet demand for each of the top-enrolled math courses?
- What is the average number of appointments that a student needs in one term?

Processes-Related Questions
- How are multiple perspectives included in the tutor selection process?
- How much capacity does the tutoring center have to provide help desk or other on-call support to students between appointments?
- How does the tutoring center train tutors about various learning styles?

Outcomes-Related Questions
- How can the students' course performance data be used to adjust the intake process?
- How can highly skilled and successful tutors help the center with yearly planning activities?

Actual Campus Example—Improving Students' Access to the Campus Recreation Center

Sean Basso from the University of Tennessee (personal communication, December 19, 2019) works in the campus recreation center and explains, in the following quote, how he used data to help address an issue of overcrowding in the facility:

Rec Center Usage

We track people swiping into our recreation center and there was a much higher percentage for them reporting that our facility was overcrowded than the national and regional averages. Most people's response to that is strategically planning and how to expand space or reallocate space accordingly. We're pretty limited in that regard. So, as an enthusiast of physics, I know that space and time are tied. So, I tapped into the time element of it and I looked at the way the masses were coming and students are swiping in, all at the same time, all between 5 and 9 or 10 o'clock and it was creating a bottleneck. So, I said what if we were to educate the student masses about this phenomena because they're saying we're overcrowded and obviously have to enter the facility to know that it's overcrowded. So, I took the time to actually calculate projected participation patterns throughout the year on a day-to-day basis. Then, I had a marketing and graphic design student bring a data display to life on a 20 foot long, 10 foot high billboard that hung inside the turnstiles.

I put every one of those line graphs from hour to hour in projected data up to say if you plan to come next Thursday, or if you plan to come two Tuesdays from now, this is the way we project the foot traffic in the building to look like. So, I put it up at the beginning of the semester and kind of eyeballed it from time to time to see if people were looking at it. Every once in a while, I'd see a group of students gathered around it and looking at it. The semester went on and I went back and plotted against the projection what the behavior actually ended up being and it ended up altering it pretty significantly where we saw more students coming in the morning and more coming in at noon. So, the students that had expressed that there was an overcrowding issue altered their behavior so that they didn't feel overcrowded in the building. They were able to get their workout in throughout the day which ultimately helped everybody because we were having this issue. That was a positive takeaway from a really laborious data exercise that I had to go through to get that information out to our students.

Example 2: Using Data to Improve Students' Access to Practitioner-Delivered Resources

As today's students manage multiple obligations, it is crucial for institutions to provide resources that are as easy to access as possible. For example, with regard to adult learners, Wesley (2018) states that investment in robust program evaluation efforts will help institutions better understand the depth and breadth of these students' experiences and identify effective practices to serve them. Such approaches as sequencing students' appointments with academic and financial coaches will help students with the timing of several important and connected actions, such as completing the FAFSA and selecting an internship for which to apply.

A practice example relates to how a campus registrar can examine how class start times align with public transportation schedules. For institutions that are located in areas that have a city bus or metro railway service, some students will use those to commute to campus and some institutions have partnerships with the local transit authority to provide low- or no-cost fares. While this is certainly a good option, in some instances, the public transportation schedule might not be optimally aligned with students' course schedules. The specific tactic for this practice example is related to determining the extent to which course start times are within 15 minutes of public transportation arrival times to the campus.

In this example, the registrar could leverage the Research and Analysis component of their data identity by creating a spreadsheet of times for when each type of public transportation arrives and departs the campus. The registrar could then compare that to the start and end times for each course, the average walk time from the public transit campus location to the farthest campus building in which courses are held, and the schedule for the campus bus, if one is available. These simple data points will provide context for the actual time necessary for students to arrive for their classes.

Addressing Relevant Needs, Processes, and Outcomes

Similar to Example 1, the goal in this scenario is to examine how a current structure is impacting operations. The following questions can help professionals check the status of various needs and processes to identify necessary adjustments.

Needs-Related Questions

- Which, if any, courses end at a time that would require students to wait longer than one hour before the next arrival time for public transportation?
- Are there students, such as those with physical disabilities, who would be especially challenged by misaligned course and transportation schedules?

Process-Related Questions

- Which, if any, course times could be adjusted in a future term to make the alignment smoother?
- For courses that start less than 15 minutes after the arrival time for public transportation, how can those be flagged in the course registration system?

Outcomes-Related Questions

- How does a misalignment between public transportation schedules and course start times hinder students' ability to register for the courses they need and thus stay on pace?
- How could the results of the examination inform future conversations with the public transit authority about route schedules?

Example 3: Using Data to Address Students' Personal Connections

For many students, especially those who are in their first year, a welcoming college environment is vital to their overall success, as decades of research confirms that students who are actively engaged with their campus have higher rates of persistence (Astin, 1975; Kuh, 1995). For many years, professionals have managed programs that foster students' connections with each other. Such approaches include placing students with the same major of study in orientation courses together and developing clubs and activities for students who may be attending college from far away homes.

A practice example could address how an assistant director of online learning at a fully online institution can help assess the impact of a virtual peer mentoring program. Colvin and Ashman (2010) state that peer mentoring is a type of relationship in which a more experienced student helps a less experienced student and provides advice, support, and knowledge to the mentee. For institutions that primarily provide courses, supplemental instruction, and support resources in an online environment, there still exists a need for students to form connections and learn from each other. The specific action for this practice example is to evaluate students' perceptions of virtual peer engagement to learn essential skills and navigate the college environment.

Online peer Mentors

Addressing Relevant Needs, Processes, and Outcomes

The Industry Context component of the data identity framework is especially relevant for this example, as the assistant director could review approaches from other fully online institutions and survey students about the themes from the background review. As with any original data collection, the professional should collaborate with colleagues to develop a purposeful instrument.

Needs-Related Questions
- To what extent is the program helping students who need mentors with certain skills such as bilingual ability?
- How do students' mentoring needs vary by year of study?

Process-Related Questions
- How are peer mentors trained to direct students who need services, such as mental health counseling, to the appropriate campus personnel?
- How does the online peer mentoring process ensure that sensitive information is protected?

Outcomes-Related Questions
- How can the peer mentoring survey results inform other campus engagement efforts?
- To what extent do students consider the peer mentoring experience helpful to their progress in college?

Actual Campus Example—Addressing First-Year Student Engagement
The following quote from John Jones from the University of Alabama at Birmingham (personal communication, November 5, 2019) provides

an actual example of how he used data to prioritize an important type of support for students: *engage parents/family*

Around 2015, the president made the decision to bring back the division of student affairs. Consequently, I was hired in the role to lead that division. So, coming on board, there are many priorities but the emphasis at the time was student engagement and the student environment specifically in terms of fostering a sense of belonging. So, I had to make some decisions about what departments, staffing, and positions to prioritize and hire first in looking at our five-year plan. One of the things I did was look at the National Survey of Student Engagement (NSSE) data and what I saw was that sophomore students were a bit more engaged than our freshman students.

As I started analyzing that, one department that I thought it was important early on to create and staff was parents and family services. What more can we do to transition our new full-time freshman students into the campus population as well as, seeing that a significant number of our students are first generation college students, what can we do to also transition the parents to their son, daughter, or family member being a student? What information and resources can we use to help them understand what happens on college campuses as well as ensure that our students are being connected to the resources and then taking advantage of the resources? So, creating and staffing that parents and family services department as well as giving them the resources in terms of programming was based largely on the NSSE data.

Example 4: Using Data to Inform Policies and Practices

In advocating for institutions to examine how credit for prior learning can help students' progress, D'Amico et al. (2019) state that having a policy in place and enacting practice are two separate issues. However, one could argue that while policy and practice are indeed separate things, campus policies are often tethered to campus practices in myriad ways. In some instances, a well-structured policy provides a structure for institutions to consistently deliver effective practices. In other situations, a timely and innovative practice may lead a campus to adjust a long-standing policy to better address students' needs. Whether policy precedes practice or follows it, there is ample opportunity for professionals to use data to ensure that effective campus practices are supported with thoughtful and purposeful policies.

The following practice example addresses how a financial aid coordinator can examine students' financial literacy regarding student loans. The issue of student loan indebtedness is timely, as the Federal

Reserve Bank (Board of Governors of the Federal Reserve System, 2019) surveyed 10,000 individuals in the United States and found that 54% of young adults who attended college had debt, including student loans, for their education, and in 2018, 20% of those who still owed money were behind on their repayment. The specific action in this example is related to determining the extent to which students who have acquired loans understand their repayment obligations.

In this scenario, the financial aid coordinator can leverage the Curiosity and Inquiry and Communication and Consultation portions of their data identity. For practice purposes, this example assumes that the professional has a developing level of ability which, as described in chapter 2, involves identifying details that are different from the norm and framing initial ideas about what is happening. The financial aid coordinator can build on their inquiry by talking with colleagues who coach or advise students, especially those who conduct exit loan counseling to soon-to-be graduates.

financial literacy

Addressing Relevant Needs, Processes, and Outcomes

One step the financial aid coordinator can take is to gather students' frequently asked questions and suggest how to strategically pair academic and financial information for students. The following questions would help the professional identify additional steps to improve communications.

Needs-Related Questions

- What percentage of currently enrolled students have acquired loans for two or more consecutive quarters or semesters but have not attended a financial aid counseling session?
- To what extent are loan documents supplemented with information that is easy for students to understand?

Process-Related Questions

- How much information about loan repayment is provided to students at the time each loan is disbursed?
- What kinds of incentives can the financial aid office offer to entice students to learn about the loan repayment process?

Outcomes-Related Questions

- How can the institution use information about students' awareness of repayment to adjust practices?
- What percentage of students who have paused enrollment also have student loans for at least two terms?

Actual Campus Example—Advising Policy as a Lever for Student Retention
Claire Robinson at the University of South Carolina (personal communication, January 16, 2020) describes an experience from a prior institution in which a decade of longitudinal data showed the long-term impact of a data-informed change to a campus policy:

Probation coaching USC

Earlier in my career, we started seeing some trends related to students on academic probation. Academic probation on our campus was defined as having below a 2.0 grade point average and we were specifically looking at freshman year. It happened to coincide with some federal mandates regarding satisfactory academic progress. So, students that receive federal aid have to make satisfactory academic progress towards their degree. We ran all kinds of data analyses on these students. We took a look at the number of students who fell into that category, where they were skewed, and certain majors. Then, we put forth a proposal to faculty senate that said here's the need, here's the students, here's what we're proposing. Basically, we wanted to mandate some academic coaching while in probationary status.

Ten years later, we have data that shows that students who were coached within the first six weeks of the subsequent semester of being placed on probation have statistically significant higher grade point averages than those who were coached after the six-week mark or weren't coached at all. So, we used data to inform that policy proposal that then was passed by faculty senate and then had 10 years of longitudinal data that showed how that one policy and decision has made a positive impact on student retention.

Example 5: Using Data to Tailor Teaching and Learning Experiences

Students spend more time in class-based learning environments than in any other learning space, and as institutions monitor course completions and persistence toward a credential, it is essential for professionals to explore new ways to enhance students' learning experiences. For example, Ajlen et al. (2020) examined the use of gameful pedagogy as a method by which professors can transform their courses and motivate students to learn in a new way. Gameful pedagogy is defined as an approach that takes inspiration from well-designed games to create learning environments that support student motivation (Holman, 2018).

Ajlen et al. state that two important aspects of gameful pedagogy are that it provides opportunities for students to build competence through authenticity and choose how they demonstrate learning, including how they recover should an instance of underperformance occur. It is likely that such an approach to teaching and learning requires significant intentionality from instructors in the course design. Common approaches for measuring the impact of pedagogy include the use of institution-developed course evaluations and other surveys of students. The following practice example focuses on how an adjunct instructor could use data to identify culturally relevant course material. The specific action is related to gathering students' feedback on the extent to which course reading assignments are related to their lived experiences.

In this example, the instructor could leverage the Strategy and Planning component of their data identity. Their role likely requires frequent interaction with students regarding course material, which informs the approach to assessing the cultural relevance of assignments. The instructor could start by gathering qualitative data about how students perceive connections between the existing course materials and their personal experiences, interests, background, and overall academic progression. The instructor could ask students to share, if they are comfortable, instances when course material has triggered a negative emotion or sparked a fond personal memory. The instructor should also ask students to suggest how the structure of the course could be modified to help them feel more comfortable participating in discussions.

Culturally relevant teaching

Addressing Relevant Needs, Processes, and Outcomes

This example can be applied to both online and in-person class settings, as the instructor in any setting will have opportunities to gather information directly from students. Based on the feedback from the students, the professional could proceed with the following questions.

Needs-Related Questions

- How are students from diverse backgrounds reacting to course material?
- What additional investment in course resources is needed to meet students' expectations?

Process-Related Questions

- How often is the course syllabus updated to include culturally relevant material?
- How are course materials selected?

Outcomes-Related Questions

- How will students' feedback be shared with other faculty in the department?
- How can adjustments to the syllabus improve the learning objectives for the course?

Actual Campus Example—Real-Time Responses to Students

In the following quote, Tim Bono (personal communication, October 23, 2019) describes several ways in which he uses data to tailor his delivery of material and identify when students need additional help:

> When it comes to my teaching, I use data in a variety of ways. For example, I calculate item statistics for each exam that I administer. Seeing how many students answer each item correctly helps me understand which questions seem to be the best at gauging student learning, and which topics I might need to teach differently in the future. Such analyses can also give me a sense of which students are coming to class and which students are more engaged overall.
>
> I also collect data in real time during class. There are a number of mobile device response platforms that allow students to respond to questions I pose during lecture, allowing me to measure immediately their level of understanding. If we are covering a particular idea or theory in class, I can create a question on the fly, such as, "Which of the following theories is most appropriate to address this particular research question?" This way, I can see instantly if there are particular topics I need to spend more time on. If 95% of the students get that answer correct, I might take a moment to clarify things for the remaining 5%, but I know we're mostly good to keep moving on. If only 10% of the students get it correct, I know I need to go back and thoroughly revisit that material because there's clearly some uncertainty there.
>
> Another way that I collect data is by having students write weekly thought papers. That also provides a lot of useful information. Such qualitative data helps me understand what aspects of the class they are engaging in most meaningfully, and also where there might be some confusion with a given topic. For example, if students are misusing terminology or confusing concepts we have covered, I know I need to go back and correct course to ensure they have a good grasp on the material moving forward.

Example 6: Using Data to Integrate Learning Experiences

Learning happens in a variety of college settings, and as institutions strive to join curricular and cocurricular learning more intentionally, the focus on integrated learning is now more relevant than ever. For example, Northeastern University (n.d.) developed the self-authored integrated learning (SAIL) framework, which is described as the foundation for a community where learning happens everywhere. Students at the university are introduced to the five SAIL components: intellectual agility, global mindset, social consciousness and commitment, professional and personal effectiveness, and well-being.

This type of focus on the connections between learning domains is prevalent at many institutions across the United States. The final chapter of this book will address how more campuses will use data in the future to measure the extent to which integrated learning is occurring in settings such as living learning communities and internships. The following practice example focuses on how a faculty member can address the process by which students identify skills and competencies gained from service learning. The specific action is related to helping students connect the competencies gained in their out-of-classroom service to classroom material.

In this scenario, the faculty member can leverage the Industry Context component of their data identity. Similar to the earlier example related to peer mentoring, the professional can gather information about existing frameworks that campuses use across the United States to measure learning that occurs in multiple spaces. The faculty member could start by reviewing existing resources such as the widely referenced Essential Learning Outcomes, which the Association of American Colleges & Universities (n.d.-a) describes as a set of domains that students need to be ready for 21st century challenges. The faculty member could then review the rubrics associated with the Essential Learning Outcomes, one of which is related to personal and social responsibility with a focus on civic engagement (Association of American Colleges & Universities, n.d.-b).

Service learning SLO

Addressing Relevant Needs, Processes, and Outcomes

Following the review of these materials, a good next step would be to develop a course assignment using the learning outcomes that requires students to reflect on their learning. One example is the use of an e-Portfolio, a high-impact practice that allows students to explain the depth and breadth of what they know and can do. The e-Portfolio would help students narrate their service experience and demonstrate their learning in a unique and creative way. The following questions would help with planning and using an e-Portfolio to help students connect their learning.

Needs-Related Questions
- What is students' level of comfort with using a web-based resource to describe their learning?
- What investment, if any, is required from the department or students to use an e-Portfolio?

Process-Related Questions
- What types of reflection exercises can help students connect out-of-classroom and classroom-based learning?
- What additional frameworks or rubrics should be reviewed to assess students' learning?

Outcomes-Related Questions
- How can the students retain access to their e-Portfolio after the course is completed?
- What value does the e-Portfolio provide for students as they prepare for employment and other opportunities?

Example 7: Using Data to Improve Family-Focused Programming

For many students, especially those who are the first in their family to attend college, the experience of entering a new learning environment can be both exciting and overwhelming. As a result, it is common for institutions to develop family orientation sessions and, in the instance of the University of Montana (n.d.), an official newsletter for families of enrolled students. The following practice example focuses on family programming by addressing how an assistant director of campus life can learn more about the needs of student parents. Student parents have been a focus for institutions for years, as the U.S. Department of Education provides grant funding to institutions through the Child Care Access Means Parents in School (CCAMPIS) program. The program, which provides campus-based child care services to low-income parents in college, can be used for before- and after-school services (U.S. Department of Education, n.d.-a). The specific action is related to examining the extent to which student parents feel the institution's programming efforts are meeting their needs.

The assistant director in this example can leverage the Research and Analysis component of their data identity and use an approach that starts with gathering as much relevant information as possible about student parents on their campus. The information would include such data as the number of students who have reported having dependents. If the campus is residential and provides family housing, additional data about the average number of students who have lived there would also provide useful context. After reviewing that information, the professional could select a sample of student parents and invite them to participate in a focus group, one in which they can bring their children and get to know each other.

Addressing Relevant Needs, Processes, and Outcomes

As the assistant director in this example prepares for the focus groups, the following questions would help assess how well the campus is addressing student parents' needs. Depending on the number of students who agree to participate, the professional may need to invite a colleague to join the conversation, both to help capture students' reflections and to bring additional perspectives to the discussion.

[handwritten margin note: parenting students - childcare]

Needs-Related Questions
- In addition to caring for a dependent child, what other noncollege obligations are students managing that would impact their ability to participate in campus offerings?
- To what extent are student parents able to use existing campus resources to find and communicate with each other?

Process-Related Questions
- How are resources for student parents connected to other campus programs for ease of access?
- How can the campus differentiate programming for student parents to acknowledge and affirm their unique attributes?

Outcomes-Related Questions
- How does the institution's current personnel and financial investment in student parent programming compare to that for other student populations?
- What percentage of currently enrolled student parents are on pace to complete a credential without delays?

Example 8: Using Data to Simplify Complex Administrative Tasks for Students

Institutions can make it easier for students to navigate the college experience by continuously finding ways to make required actions simpler. For example, the United States Government Accountability Office (GAC, 2019) examined options for how college students could access federal food assistance benefits such as those from the Supplemental Nutrition Assistance Program (SNAP). One recommendation from the GAO was for the Food and Nutrition Service (FNS) to make information on their website regarding students' eligibility requirements easier to understand and more accessible, which would be a resource for colleges (United States Government Accountability Office, 2019). Although this recommendation is primarily directed to a government office, it is relevant to campuses in that the end goal is the same, which is to make required processes as clear as possible. Tactical approaches for simplifying administrative tasks include reducing the number of steps to register for courses and attain a student identification card. The following practice example addresses how a director of the career center can use data to help improve the on-campus employment program.

The specific action is related to improving the methods by which students can apply for available positions.

In this example, the director can leverage the Campus Context component of their data identity. As mentioned in chapter 3, Burnside et al. (2019) conducted a national study of on-campus employment programs, which included both Federal Work–Study positions and those funded by institutional investment. Their research suggests that the most important type of outreach for students who are interested in on-campus employment is a central location for all available positions, as it would help students who do not have personal connections from whom they can find out about jobs (Burnside et al., 2019). This example assumes that the director works at a campus that has a central job listing online. A good first step is for the director to review the listing, select a position, and calculate the time necessary to complete all steps of the application process. A second step would be for the director to ask a student to review a sample of job listings and note any terms or references that are unclear. Following those two steps, the director could prepare a survey for colleagues in various departments that have positions listed. The focus of the survey is to identify how the selection process varies by department.

On campus employment

Addressing Relevant Needs, Processes, and Outcomes

Considering the high number of students who are working while in college, this example is especially timely. As a result of the director's actions, the process for students to apply for campus jobs should become much easier. The following questions will help with the last step of constructing a survey of colleagues to find ways to give students a smooth job search process.

Needs-Related Questions
- What is the range in level of prior experience or skills needed for entry-level on-campus job postings?
- How does the amount of supervision and direct coaching available vary by position?

Process-Related Questions
- How are divisions and departments informing students about the availability of the job listing?
- How can the career center help students prepare for on-campus employment interviews and actual jobs?

Outcomes-Related Questions
- What percentage of students who have worked in an on-campus position for consecutive years have received an increase in pay or level of responsibility?
- If the online listing has a feature that allows applicants to save portions of the application, at what rate are students starting an application but not submitting it?

Example 9: Using Data to Improve Resource Allocation

In their study of how institutions use data and analytics, Parnell et al. (2018) found that the leading reason was to improve student outcomes, followed by more efficient delivery of programs and services, as mentioned in the start of the chapter. The third leading reason was to eliminate or reduce programs shown to not contribute significantly to student success, which 39% of institutional research, information technology, and student affairs professionals reported as an institutional goal. One purpose of improving resource allocation is to reduce costly expenses, which some campuses approach by merging programs with similar focus areas or changing the frequency of when a service is delivered.

The following quote from Anthony DeSantis at Florida International University (personal communication, December 23, 2019) describes how some institutions might use data to improve resource allocation:

> We're getting ready for activity and service budget proposals and our student government body is making decisions based upon student success and institutional affinity. They want to know if our students are being successful in the programs that they're giving us money for so all of our assessment data has to be linked to these factors. If we can't show that, then they're not going to give us the money. So, I think everything we do today has some type of data link to it.

The following practice example addresses how a director of campus activities can use data to plan how the campus can sponsor a select number of campus speakers for the upcoming academic year. The specific action is related to selecting a group of speakers who will appeal to students' interests while reducing the overall spending by 35%.

In this example, the director can leverage the Communication and Consultation component of their data identity. The task of identifying efficiencies while meeting students' expectations will not be easy, but it is attainable. The first step for the director is to identify the leading cost drivers, which are likely the speakers' fees and logistics costs for the speakers to visit the campus in person. The next step is to review any post-event evaluations from prior speakers with a focus on how students rated the in-person aspects of the experience. The last step is to consult with a group of students, perhaps from the student government association, to gather a list of topics of most importance to the general population. *Campus speaker series*

Addressing Needs, Processes, and Outcomes

Following these steps, the director can devise a plan that would result in a mix of in-person and virtual guest speakers, to cover both the need for speakers on relevant topics and the reduced spending from fewer in-person travel expenses. The following questions could assist the director in creating a set of action steps to execute the plan.

Needs-Related Questions
- How will the institution ensure that the virtual gatherings can accommodate any students with hearing or visual impairments?
- How do topics of interest for public speakers vary by student demographics?

Process-Related Questions
- How can a virtual gathering include opportunities for students to engage with the speaker in a meet and greet format following the event?
- What types of post-event activities can the campus offer to continue discussions of the material?

Outcome-Related Questions
- How does the selection of speakers connect to the institution's strategic goals?
- How does students' attendance at the in-person events compare to that of the virtual events?

Example 10: Using Data to Identify Professionals' Learning Needs

For higher education professionals who are committed to lifelong learning and ongoing professional development, there are countless topics for which additional training can be useful. For example, the Council for the Advancement of Standards in Higher Education (2019) recently released the 10th edition of a set of general standards which address the essential components and characteristics of quality programs and services. These standards, which are divided into 12 parts, include areas such as human resources; communication and collaboration; ethics, law, and policy; student learning, development, and success; assessment; and several other topics.

Tactical approaches to professional development include investing in webinars, live briefings, and in-person institutes and conferences. The following practice example focuses on how a director of campus communications can develop a division-wide training on effective use of email messages to students. The specific action is related to helping colleagues develop purposeful email messages for students who have been identified as being close to not meeting satisfactory academic progress.

For this example, the director can leverage the Campus Context and Strategy and Planning components of their data identity. The primary purpose of the division-wide training is to help administrators develop a more structured approach for communicating with students via email. The director would certainly need to address operational aspects of a well-organized communication plan but, for the purposes of this example, the focus is on identifying professionals' individual training needs. The first step the director can take is to converse with colleagues in the division to gauge their knowledge of effective email strategies. The goal is not to highlight professionals' deficiencies but instead to identify which training topics are most needed. The next step is to review a sample of email messages that have been sent to students and note the varying purposes, such as those that were sent to inform and those that were sent as a reminder to take action. After completing those steps, the director could conduct a few focus groups of students with varying classification levels and backgrounds.

Addressing Relevant Needs, Processes, and Outcomes

The director's conversations with colleagues, review of prior messages, and student focus groups will provide a balanced approach for delivering a useful training session. One commonly used statement is that students do not read their email messages. If this is true, the time investment will be worth it in the long term, because it could help professionals reduce the number of messages, develop more tailored information, and possibly impact students' behaviors. The following additional questions would help the director prepare for the training experience.

Needs-Related Questions
- What proportion of staff have participated in a prior training related to effective email communication?
- To what extent do professionals in the division understand the varying factors that can hinder students' academic progress?

Process-Related Questions
- For the messages that were previously sent to remind students to take an action, did the instructions include contact information for someone who could answer questions?
- What steps can the division take to promote the use of affirming language rather than deficit-based language?

Outcomes-Related Questions
- How does the open rate for email messages sent to students from the division compare to that of messages sent from the campus communications office?
- For messages that include a hyperlink to a campus resource webpage, at what rate do students visit the hyperlink?

Additional Considerations

While each of the previous examples describes an opportunity to align programs and services with students' needs, professionals should remember two things that can impact the coordination and execution of their work. The first is the volume of requests that students receive. As faculty, administrators, and staff seek students' opinions, it is important to not create a burden with too many new data collections. For example, rather than ask all students to participate in new data collections, one might consider how a representative sample of students can achieve the same goal. A second consideration is the balance of necessary versus interesting analyses. As mentioned in chapter 2, the Curiosity and Inquiry component of one's data identity is helpful in that it requires an initial focus on existing data and information. In some instances, determining whether the outcome of a potential analysis would be useful to know or simply interesting can save time and resources that can be better applied elsewhere.

Conclusion

From resource allocations to making facilities more accessible, there are countless ways for professionals to use data to give students optimal programs and services. The examples provided in this chapter highlight a need to balance tailoring services to individual students with achieving a replicable level of scale. The following quote from Jonathan Gagliardi at Lehman

College (personal communication, December 17, 2019) describes the potential for data-informed approaches to program and service delivery:

> We have some programs that offer a lot of rich qualitative information about the student experience that frankly would give us a lot more than quantitative data. I'd like to see us as a community spend more time hearing, reading, and listening so that we can either continue to build out the quality services we have or pivot resources in ways that actually help the highest proportion of our students. So, we've got to think about quality, we've got to think about impact, we've got to think about scale, and we've got to think about student needs for a very distinctive and segmented student population.

Although data-informed strategies can be difficult, especially when conditions are changing, if professionals collaborate and share their knowledge of campus and industry contexts, maintain a focus on needs, processes, and outcomes, and continue listening to students, their programs and services will be the best possible. The next chapter continues the focus on practical examples with 10 ways that professionals can use data to monitor and address students' progress.

6

DATA IN ACTION PART 2: 10 WAYS TO USE DATA TO MONITOR AND ADDRESS STUDENTS' PROGRESS

Right now, and I think moving forward in the next five years, there will still be a lot of emphasis on big data. There will be a more heightened sense of the different analytical tools and resources that folks can get access to so they can figure out how to better serve their institutional mission and their students' needs. Whole programs of study are being redesigned and I think some of that redesign is going to be based on how people are looking at student needs based on their use of analytics.

—Eboni Zamani-Gallaher, University of Illinois at Urbana-Champaign

Although the previous quote (E. Zamani-Gallaher, personal communication, January 13, 2020) offers a prediction of the future of data use in higher education, which will be addressed in chapter 8, the context of the comment is especially relevant to today's students. The use of data to address students' progress is now a high priority as institutions realize the vast ways that students' needs intersect. This chapter provides 10 examples that professionals can consider when monitoring students' progress. The focus is on a variety of student behaviors that could be leading indicators of their level of financial or academic stability or acclimation to the college environment.

During the background interviews for this book, professionals were asked to describe something on their data wish list. The wish list was described as a topic or idea that the professional perceived as timely but had not yet examined at great length. A few of those reflections are also included in this chapter. As with chapter 5, this chapter references research studies and reports, includes discussion questions to examine needs and improve processes, and describes how one can use various components of their data identity to collaborate with others. The following examples are not intended to solve exact problems but instead to spark discussions about how certain trends could be relevant to one's own campus.

Example 1: Housing Insecurity

Campus health and wellness centers are a resource for students to both learn and address their physical, social, and emotional needs. These centers, which have programs ranging from instructor-led classes such as yoga and Pilates to self-guided fitness equipment, typically have operating hours that allow students to enter early in the morning and depart late at night. While some students may prefer to visit the center at off-peak hours because it fits their daily schedule, other students may do so for reasons that could impact their progress in college. In some instances, students may choose to visit the center during off-peak hours because of a housing challenge. Visiting the center early in the morning or late at night would allow students more discretion to use shower facilities and take other actions to manage a housing displacement.

Hallett and Crutchfield (2017) state that the majority of U.S. colleges and universities do not collect or report data concerning residential status. However, research is emerging that indicates some college students are experiencing housing challenges that range from housing instability to homelessness. For example, Crutchfield et al. (2016) conducted a system-wide study of institutions in the California State University (CSU) system and preliminarily found that approximately 12% of CSU students experienced homelessness and housing insecurity. With regard to off-peak visits to the health and wellness center, a student affairs professional could leverage the Curiosity and Inquiry component of their data identity to discuss the following questions with colleagues.

- How does the institution direct students to housing support services?
- If the campus has gathered survey data or other information regarding students' housing status, how do rates of housing instability vary by student classification and other demographics?

Example 2: Change to Payment Method

DeSantis and Glezerman (2013) state that with regard to payment of charges, institutions typically decide by term whether the full amount will be due and how to accommodate students who cannot pay the full amount. For students who receive federal financial aid, much of the process of applying the aid to charges incurred is managed by the institution, as the funds are typically disbursed to the campus to be applied to a student's account balance. For students whose expenses are not fully covered by outside aid and are responsible for making payments to the institution, a change in method of payment could indicate an underlying financial issue.

Not every student who changes their method of paying their account balance from a debit-based option to a credit-based option is experiencing financial instability. However, some students who change methods, especially those who do not qualify for need-based aid, could be close to experiencing significant financial distress. Administrative professionals could leverage the Research and Analysis component of their data identity to engage with colleagues about the following questions to proactively help students.

- What percentage of students who pay with a different method each semester have also paused taking courses following a previous academic term?
- How are students informed about flexible options for paying their account balances?

Example 3: Partial Meal Plan Purchase

Kruger et al. (2016) found over 500 institutions that offer emergency aid to students, and of those more than 50% of public two- and four-year institutions were addressing food insecurity. These figures underscore the relevance of the issue, but research also revealed that more work is needed, as word of mouth is the primary method by which students learn about the availability of aid (Kruger et al., 2016). Some campuses give students the option to select from a set of meal plan options that include purchasing all meals that are available or a portion of total meals available. For students who live on campus, the choice to not purchase the full meal plan could be simply a matter of preference. But, for other students, it could be a financial issue that contributes to food insecurity.

It is important to note that the issue of food insecurity may not be exclusively related to students who have lower incomes. For example, students who do not quality for any need-based aid but whose family cannot support the full cost of college may also struggle with meeting basic needs. Food insecurity is an issue that professionals across an institution can address with the Campus Context component of their data identity and the following discussion questions.

- How is the institution informing students about available resources such as the food pantry via multiple channels such as social media, email, course syllabi, and coaching or advising sessions?
- What percentage of students who are not purchasing the full meal plan also do not have an on-campus job?

Example 4: FAFSA Completion

For low-income students, acquiring financial aid is essential to their progress toward completing a credential. The FAFSA is the primary method by which students can determine their eligibility for grants, loans, and scholarships. Completing the FAFSA is required to receive most types of need-based aid, yet research suggests that some students may not fully understand the process. For example, Coker and Glynn (2017) state that students are not always aware that the FAFSA must be completed each year in order to continue receiving need-based aid and advise institutions to remind students of the requirement.

Considering the impact that not completing the FAFSA can have on students' persistence, professionals should monitor it proactively and on an ongoing basis. Financial aid administrators can leverage the Strategy and Planning component of their data identity to discuss the following questions with colleagues.

- What percentage of students who are not completing the FAFSA on time are also not regularly engaging with other support services such as advising?
- To what extent are reminders about FAFSA completion intentionally connected to other required actions such as registering for courses?

Example 5: Inactive Use of Identification Card

Burke et al. (2017) examined how institutions are using data to anticipate student behaviors and found that some institutions monitor the rates at which students use their campus identification card to access a program or service within a certain period of time. For example, if a student has not used their identification card within the first few weeks of the academic term, it could indicate an intention to depart from the institution or inability to access resources. A professional in the campus administration office could leverage the Communication and Consultation component of their data identity to learn more about what, if any, challenges students might be experiencing. The following questions can aid a discussion with colleagues.

- What percentage of first-generation students are not using their identification card regularly?
- What percentage of students who are not using their identification card to access services are also not logging into the learning management system regularly?

Example 6: Transcript Requests

Burke et al. (2017) also found that some institutions review characteristics of students who request an official copy of their academic transcript. It is not uncommon for students to request a transcript near the completion of their credential. However, it is possible that a student who is making satisfactory academic progress but not close to completing a credential is requesting a copy of the transcript in order to transfer to another institution. Burke et al. (2017) reported that at the time of the transcript request, institutions can prompt a student to have a discussion with an academic counselor to discuss their experience with the institution.

When asked about an item on his data wish list, Garrett Smith at the University of Massachusetts Boston (personal communication, January 14, 2020) described the elusive question of why students depart an institution:

> One thing that jumps right to mind is why our students leave us. Our six-year graduation rate for first-time full-time freshmen is about 50%. So, 50% leave and it's really hard to figure out why and what we should do about it. We can go into the National Student Clearinghouse and pull data and see who transferred and where they transferred to. We can see who had holds on their account and whether it was financial or advising or whether they had poor grades. We can gather a bunch of data but we just don't know exactly why they leave and most students don't formally withdraw. So, even when we ask and get some students to fill out the withdrawal form, it's still hard to figure out and it's vague or a combination of reasons. The majority of students never give us any information.

An academic adviser could leverage the Campus Context component of their identity in this scenario and discuss the following questions with colleagues.

- What percentage of students request a transcript with less than 50% of credential requirements completed?
- At what rate did students who requested a transcript also use campus support services such as career or academic advising?

Example 7: Accessing the Learning Management System

Similar to the example regarding students' use of their campus identification card, monitoring the rates at which students access the learning management system (LMS) could also reveal aspects of their progress. Galanek et al. (2018) state that even basic LMS functions such as posting grades contribute to a student's academic performance, as they provide real-time monitoring of their course progress and the opportunity to make any midcourse adjustments that are needed. Of the more than 50,000 students who were surveyed for their research, more than three-fourths reported that the LMS was used for most or all of their courses (Galanek et al., 2018).

Considering institutions' high reliance on LMS platforms to deliver high-quality course experiences, it is essential for students to be actively engaged with the system to keep pace with material. By proactively examining the levels at which students are accessing the LMS, professionals can identify students who may need additional support. Those who regularly deliver content to the LMS can leverage the Communication and Consulting component of their data identity to discuss the following questions with colleagues.

- What percentage of students who are not accessing the LMS are also not accessing their campus email account?
- How do the rates of students accessing the LMS vary by student classification and major of study?

Example 8: Changes to Mailing Address

Similar to the example related to off-peak usage of the health and wellness center, another possible indicator of housing instability is the rate at which students change their on-file mailing address. The U.S. Department of Education's Office of Federal Student Aid (FSA) states that students who are completing the FAFSA must provide a mailing address where they can reliably receive mail (U.S. Department of Education Office of Federal Student Aid, 2020). If students consistently change the mailing address for this process or another required action, it could be an indicator that the student is experiencing a housing challenge.

Considering the sensitive nature of this issue, it is important for professionals to use careful judgement when examining students' housing status. Rather than rush into gathering new information, a good first step for one to take is to leverage the Campus Context component of their data identity and discuss the following questions with a colleague.

- What percentage of students who have changed their mailing address more than once in an academic term have also requested emergency aid resources?
- What percentage of students who have changed their mailing address more than once in an academic term are on pace to complete a credential without delays?

This example could also be relevant to students who do not have a parent or guardian. For example, Sarubbi (2019) states that campuses should offer year-round housing options to meet diverse student needs, which include foster care alumni and other students who do not have a parent or guardian with whom to live between academic terms.

Example 9: Cocurricular Engagement

As mentioned in the previous chapter, students have a variety of out-of-classroom environments in which they can learn and increase their connection to others and the institution. The research on high-impact practices (HIPs) such as undergraduate research, service learning, and collaborative assignments and projects suggests that these engagements elevate students' performance on desired outcomes (Kuh, 2008; NSSE, 2007), and Kinzie (2012) states that most HIPs can have a transformative influence on students. Institutions can use data regarding students' participation in cocurricular engagements to both improve processes and measure learning across domains. For example, in the following quote, Katherine Ziemer at Northeastern University (personal communication, December 12, 2019) described how the campus used data about students' participation in global experiences to identify which were most meaningful:

> I would say it was in prioritizing resources around our global education. One of our visions is that all of our undergraduates will have at least one international experience, one that is not just tourism but a meaningful

integrated experience. So, we did a lot of data analysis on what students did which of the variety of opportunities that we have. We meshed, as best we could, student interviews as well as patterns of what students did later, to see which were the most meaningful and put resources into those. We saw a huge increase in the number of students participating and then participating in more than one.

Campuses that connect engagement data with academic performance data can gain a better understanding of how students navigate various experiences and the extent to which those experiences impact their success. The University of Central Oklahoma is a good example, as the institution's Student Transformative Learning Record (STLR) captures students' growth and learning across six areas. Data from the record helps the campus measure the impact of various engagements on students' academic performance (University of Central Oklahoma, n.d.). Faculty and administrators can leverage the Industry Context components of their data identity and discuss the following questions related to this example.

- What percentage of transfer students are engaging in cocurricular activities?
- What are effective strategies for offering cocurricular opportunities to students at low or no cost?
- How do rates of persistence for students who participate in cocurricular activities compare to those of students who are not participating?
- What portion of cocurricular engagements provide options for students to participate during off-peak hours?

Example 10: Change of Major

When students change their major without a plan, it can result in both delayed completion of a credential and excess hours, which will increase the cost. While it is expected that some students will discover new interests and desire a different major, it is critical for students to have a clear understanding of how that decision will impact their academic and financial position. Research from Yeado et al. (2014) suggests that one way institutions can help students is by providing clear maps toward their degrees.

In some instances, students may consider changing their major for academic reasons, while in other scenarios, students may have an interest in a different career or other post-graduation goal. In both situations, professionals can help students find their ideal plan, one that maximizes their investment of time and money. Faculty and other professionals who advise students can leverage the Curiosity and Inquiry component of their data identity in this example and discuss the following questions.

- What percentage of students who change their major have participated in an internship, on-campus job, or other practical work-related experience?
- At the time a student requests a change of major, how is information shared with the student regarding the impact on their completion time and overall cost?

Additional Considerations

Professionals who intend to use data to monitor and address students' progress should be mindful of three important factors: the selection and appropriate use of technology; the effective organization and integration of data from multiple sources; and engagements with external partners such as consultants and advisers. Each of these factors can influence the level at which professionals can efficiently and responsibly use data to examine student behaviors. The following is further description of each consideration.

Selection and Appropriate Use of Technology

There is no shortage of products available in the higher education technology marketplace, which presents ample opportunity for professionals to find a resource that best fits their institution's needs. In many instances, decisions about more expensive technology investments are managed by information technology offices, as such expenditures require significant negotiations and multiyear agreements. There are several resources available to help professionals with procurement decisions, such as the Higher Education Community Vendor Assessment Toolkit (HECVAT). The HECVAT is a questionnaire framework specifically designed to help institutions measure vendor risk (EDUCAUSE, 2020a). For technology options that are less expensive and more locally deployed, professionals may wonder what criteria to use when selecting the appropriate product. Products that are affordable, easy for professionals to understand and use, and widely accessible are ideal long-term investments.

Regardless of the level of direct involvement with selecting a data collection and management tool, every professional should pair their use of technology with effective communication. Although the previous examples offer good places for which data can reveal insights into a student's journey, there are multiple factors that underlie students' behaviors. Thoughtful communication is integral to professionals understanding the nuance of students' daily experiences, as it helps prevent broad assertions or conclusions regarding students' actions. As mentioned in chapter 3, the goal is to proactively address students' progress without being overbearing.

Data Organization and Integration

There are several benefits for institutions that prioritize organizing their data across systems. Not only does organization provide a structure for more widespread data use, but it can also lead to greater integration across systems. One common challenge for institutions that have data stored in multiple and disparate systems is data definitions. The result of that challenge is that professionals in different departments could be examining data related to the same student but have different interpretations of certain variables. Therefore, it is ideal for professionals to have consistent definitions of key information to help them describe variables in similar ways. This is an opportunity for professionals to leverage the Research and Analysis part of their data identity. Even those who have an emerging ability in this area can help their campus organize and integrate data. For example, chapter 2 describes one with emerging Research and Analysis skills as being able to understand the types of data and information that are most relevant to their daily work. The additional ability to gather and organize that data, when done in collaboration with others, can help ensure that the campus conducts the most reliable analyses possible. While the step of organizing data is time-consuming and does not often yield visible outcomes, it is an essential part of effective data integration, which is a critical part of examining students' progress and outcomes. In the following quote, Pam Bowers at the University of South Carolina (personal communication, December 13, 2019) describes how the institution is improving data regarding students' cocurricular engagements:

> We're creating data. We're documenting the educational and developmental purpose and design of student affairs, academic support programs, events, and activities. We are now also documenting and recording student participation in all those programs plus programs outside of student affairs that are high-impact practices. Those are internships, study abroad, and research that is associated with courses that students receive academic credit for. We are also improving the data about those experiences and the university adopted this student affairs system to do that because we didn't have naming conventions or standards for how to define those things across the institution. Every college department kind of did things their own way so you couldn't look at institutional data and

see where all the internships were and how delivery of those internship experiences aligned with high impact practices. So, now we can do that. Although we don't have all of them in our system yet, we have made tremendous progress over the last year.

Engaging With External Partners

Consultants and advisers can provide outside perspectives to help institutions make the best use of their resources. With regard to using data to monitor students' progress, many consultants support institutions by developing algorithms, visual displays, and other tools to help professionals identify focus areas. While these engagements can be highly valuable, it is also important for professionals to remain proactive and fully understand their data. A consultant can provide the structure and resources, but those are only as effective as the end user makes it. Professionals who are new to engaging with external partners can leverage the Curiosity and Inquiry and Campus Context components of their data identity to both ask relevant questions and understand how externally developed products and services can be best applied at their campus. Jennifer Johnson at Spelman College (personal communication, November 22, 2019) offered the following example of what she would like to do after engaging with an external company:

> We have made investments in predictive analytics in an effort to improve success outcomes for our students. I have always been curious about which factors are most predictive of academic success for our population. In fact, one of my pet projects is to create a predictive retention model using campus data and data derived from alumnae, faculty, and staff insights. I want to uncover correlations between student performance and retention, and design early interventions to retain students.

Conclusion

Pusser and Levin (2009) state that the rapid pace of change in the education arena requires innovative approaches to institutional practices at every level and recommend that institutions focus on better data collection and common standards for assessing student learning and institutional effectiveness. Over a decade later, those recommendations are even more relevant, as today's higher education landscape continues to experience frequent change, and the methods by which campuses educate students must adapt as well. As professionals strive to identify the best indicators of students' success in college, the pressure to do so quickly and accurately remains. However, collaborative efforts, thoughtful approaches, and ongoing optimism can make the process of using data to proactively address students' needs a bit smoother. As Rebecca Goldstein at Florida Atlantic University (personal communication, January 17, 2020) describes as follows, professionals at all levels and across multiple offices can learn from each other:

> The culture of data use is pretty widespread and getting wider. There's a team of us that meets regularly as data professionals from institutional research, student affairs, academic affairs, financial affairs, and information technology. We meet to discuss what the trends are in our area and then how we can help each other. Those meetings are set up so that anyone who is on the teams is invited and anyone can present at any level. I've had a student intern present, a graduate student present, I have presented, and the head of the office of Institutional Effectiveness and Analysis has presented. Everyone is treated the same because you know something that we should all know. So, if someone has figured out something with one of our software (platforms), everyone can know that topic.

The next chapter resumes the focus on the data identity framework with a self-assessment exercise to help professionals identify their combination of data-related skills and abilities. The chapter also provides examples of how professionals with varying combinations of data identity components can work together to make data-informed decisions.

7

THE DATA IDENTITY SELF-ASSESSMENT EXERCISE

You can have a team approach where people come together and maybe you've got a strong communicator who's very articulate, clear, and concise and then you've got another person who has that business acumen. I don't think you can just get all of that in one person. For me, it's really that team approach. I think you can build small teams that are based on people's interests and connected to an outcome and understanding of what the expectations are.

—Helen Brewer, Rockland Community College

The previous quote (H. Brewer, personal communication, November 6, 2019) is a great description of an ideal scenario in which professionals with varying abilities contribute to a data-informed process. The references to communication and business acumen are especially relevant as they connect to the data identity framework, the set of six skills that are essential to participating in data-informed discussions, decision-making, and strategy development. Chapter 2 presented the framework and described the components, which are displayed as a reminder as follows in Figure 7.1.

This chapter features a self-assessment and five example personas to help professionals better understand their data identity. The combination of these resources is designed to show professionals the strongest parts of their identity and how various component combinations can add value to data-informed projects. As a refresher, the following are the four principles related to how the framework should be interpreted in the context of individual abilities, the value of each component, and how the skills relate to one's daily work.

1. The components are not provided in a sequential or ranking order because each is a valuable part of one's data identity.
2. Every higher education professional has some level of ability in each of the areas, even if the ability is minimal. It is expected that within

each component, some professionals will have much more experience and knowledge while others may have less exposure and knowledge. This is especially true for the Research and Analysis component. This book does not assert that every professional is ready to begin work in a full-time role that is responsible for high-priority data analysis and reporting. However, this chapter is intended to describe how nearly everyone engages in some level of work related to research and analysis and the other five areas.

3. All six components are valuable to engaging in collaborative work on a campus. This presents an opportunity for colleagues to discuss how their respective strengths can be complementary when engaging in data-informed projects together.

4. The level and frequency at which professionals engage in activities related to components will vary. While it is expected that everyone will use each component in their work to some extent, it is likely that professionals will use some components more or less often depending on their role and responsibilities.

Figure 7.1. Components of the data identity framework.

Curiosity and Inquiry	**Research and Analysis**
Ability to formulate and ask clear questions	Ability to select and use appropriate methodologies
Communication and Consultation	**Campus Context**
Ability to clearly discuss findings with multiple audiences	Knowledge of current issues and trends within the institution
Industry Context	**Strategy and Planning**
Knowledge of current issues and trends in higher education	Ability to select and execute a course of action

The Data Identity Self-Assessment

Tables 7.1 through 7.6 display the separate components of the Data Identity Self-Assessment, which contains 72 actions related to one's data identity. Each of the six components of the data identity framework has four subcomponents and an action that reflects emerging, developing, and strong ability. The exercise involves selecting the four boxes in each data identity component section, one for each subcomponent, that best reflect one's current abilities, which will result in a total of 24 self-assessment selections. Appendix A provides supplemental notes regarding the self-assessment subcomponents.

The self-assessment is designed to help professionals engage in a solo review of their data identity components. There is no overall score for the exercise, as the purpose is not to confirm whether an individual has a data identity but instead to better understand the details of it. There are certainly more activities for each ability level than the ones listed as follows. Those who desire to more closely pinpoint exact aptitudes should still refer to more formal examinations and measurements of specific skills.

In some instances, self-assessment selections will be contextual, as each person's individual experiences on a campus vary. For example, a professional may have several years of experience in higher education but recently started working in a new role at their institution or a different institution, which could impact the Campus Context component of their data identity. The emerging, developing, and strong ability ratings should be interpreted as follows:

- Professionals who have an emerging ability likely perform the listed action occasionally or at a novice level.
- Professionals who have a developing ability perform the listed action more frequently or at an increased level of responsibility.
- Professionals who have a strong ability perform the listed action on an ongoing basis or, in some instances, at a level that is consistently a model for others to follow.

Self-Assessment Instructions

Three additional principles apply to the self-assessment:

1. The ratings are as of today and should not reflect future plans or goals.
2. The ratings should be based one's individual abilities but not in the context of or in comparison to a colleague's abilities.

3. Honesty about one's abilities is critical. It is acceptable for one to have ratings that vary widely across the six components. The long-term goal of developing one's data identity is to make progress in each area, not to achieve perfection.

To complete the self-assessment exercise, one should take the following steps:

1. Read the statements in each section and for each row and related subcategory, and select the one box that best describes current ability.
2. Review all 24 selected boxes and note the components that have more self-ratings of Strong Ability or Developing Ability and which have more self-ratings of Emerging Ability.
3. Note two core components for which several Strong Ability or Developing Ability self-ratings were selected.
4. Consider how the combination of those two components can add to project work with colleagues.
5. Review the remaining components for which self-assessment ratings of Emerging Ability or Developing Ability were applied.
6. Develop a list of actions that can provide more experience for emerging or developing areas. (As a reminder, chapter 3 provides examples.)
7. Complete the self-assessment exercise again in one year.

Curiosity and Inquiry, as shown in the previous table, comprises the following subcomponent areas: issue clarity, question formulation, historical context, and stakeholder impact. Those who have abilities in this component are especially skilled at identifying topics that should be discussed as well as the people who could be most impacted.

Table 7.2 displays the subcomponent areas of Research and Analysis, which are methodology, technical expertise, data integration, and computation. Professionals who have these skills can contribute to projects that require the gathering, monitoring, and reporting of information.

Communication and Consultation is displayed in Table 7.3 and comprises the subcomponent areas of delivery type, audience, interpretation, and follow-up. The primary focus points of these subcomponents are the ability to connect issues to numerous audiences and convey relevant information using a variety of methods.

Table 7.4 displays the Campus Context subcomponents, which are: student information, programs and initiatives, strategic plan, and campus mission. Those who have abilities related to these areas can offer valuable insights about the institution's programs and services and students' experiences.

Can I do it? YES...When do I do it? RARELY

we all are
— stronger here

TABLE 7.1

Data Identity Self-Assessment Component—Curiosity and Inquiry

Curiosity and Inquiry – The Ability to Formulate and Ask Clear Questions

Subcomponent Areas	Emerging Ability	Developing Ability	Strong Ability
Issue Clarity *Skill: Identifying a problem to be addressed*	Recognize a change in a campus trend.	Determine the scope and scale of an issue across other areas of the campus.	Articulate how an issue, if unaddressed, will impact various aspects of campus operations.
Question Formation *Skill: Determining what information is needed*	Gather information that could be relevant to the cause of an issue.	Decipher between information that would be valuable to have versus information that is interesting but less useful.	Transform a list of relevant questions into a set of priority questions to be addressed.
Historical Context *Skill: Understanding relevant work that was conducted in the past*	Summarize themes from prior reports, briefs, or other resources related to an issue.	Identify results from prior projects that are relevant to a new issue.	Determine whether an issue is significant enough to pursue with a new effort or if it can be addressed with previous solutions.
Stakeholder Impact *Skill: Knowing how an issue connects to members of the campus community*	Converse with colleagues who have prior experience related to an issue.	Understand why various stakeholders would want an issue resolved.	Determine which stakeholders are most and least affected by an issue.

LOWEST – Research/curiosity

TABLE 7.2
Data Identity Self-Assessment Component—Research and Analysis

Research and Analysis—The Ability to Select and Use Appropriate Methodologies

Subcomponent Areas	Emerging Ability	Developing Ability	Strong Ability
Methodology *Skill: Determining how to address an issue with data and information*	Repurpose, with permission, a single data collection resource that is documented as applicable for researching an issue.	Consult with colleagues who have relevant experience to develop a data-informed approach for addressing an issue.	Identify, without need for guidance, the most ideal and reasonable data approach among varying options to address an issue.
Technical Expertise *Skill: Using various tools and platforms to study and display data and information*	Use resources with little customization to deliver information.	Prepare custom reports and other summaries that are visually appealing and tailored to consumers' specific needs.	Design digital, cloud-based, or online resources that colleagues can use to conduct simple analyses on their own.
Data Integration *Skill: Understanding connections among data and information from multiple sources*	Gather data from the primary systems used within an office or department.	Refer to various data dictionaries, warehouses, and databases to align data to examine an issue.	Assess weak areas of campus-wide data integration and develop processes for increasing efficiency across systems.
Computation *Skill: Using proven research methods to accurately measure outcomes*	Prepare simple calculations of data or syntheses of information.	Develop formulas and codes to produce replicable analyses of data and information.	Conduct sophisticated and advanced-level quantitative and qualitative studies of campus data trends.

TABLE 7.3

Data Identity Self-Assessment Component—Communication and Consultation

Communication and Consultation – The Ability to Clearly Discuss Findings with Multiple Audiences

Subcomponent Areas	Emerging Ability	Developing Ability	Strong Ability
Delivery Type *Skill: Sharing information in a format that is easy to understand*	Decipher when a verbal and/or written method is most applicable.	Select the appropriate amount of information to share in a variety of settings.	Explain all information using clear terms and descriptions.
Audience *Skill: Determining which information is of most interest to varying individuals*	Gather information about individuals' current work portfolios.	Provide practical examples to connect material to individuals' lived experiences.	Translate information to make a topic relevant for a variety of campus professionals.
Interpretation *Skill: Explaining myriad concerns and viewpoints in a consistent and clear manner*	Identify common interests among multiple people engaged in a discussion.	Connect ideas, perspectives, and questions across a group of colleagues involved in a discussion.	Transform multiple individual viewpoints into a cohesive narrative.
Follow-Up *Skill: Identifying opportunities for ongoing collaboration*	Maintain a list of ideas and topics for future exploration.	Share project results with new audiences to further refine conclusions.	Provide advice regarding special topics to colleagues across the institution as needs arise.

TABLE 7.4

Data Identity Self-Assessment Component—Campus Context

Campus Context – Knowledge of Current Issues and Trends Within the Institution			
Subcomponent Areas	**Emerging Ability**	**Developing Ability**	**Strong Ability**
Student Information *Skill: Understanding various characteristics of the campus student population and their progress*	Review campus fact books or other reports that contain information about student outcomes.	Engage with students who have differing backgrounds to learn about their campus experiences.	Prepare written or verbal syntheses of various student issues over multiple years.
Programs and Initiatives *Skill: Knowing how various campus activities are organized and operated*	Support activities conducted primarily by one office or unit on campus.	Participate in campus activities in collaboration with colleagues from multiple departments or divisions.	Lead institution-wide activities and, in some instances, manage relationships with external partners.
Strategic Plan *Skill: Understanding the most immediate campus priorities*	Connect individual job responsibilities to specific objectives in the campus strategic plan.	Align office or department work plans with strategic plan goals and objectives.	Manage activities that contribute to the institution's accreditation or financial stability.
Campus Mission *Skill: Working on projects that address the primary purposes for which the institution operates*	Identify how individual work addresses students' needs and progress.	Lead office or department projects that directly impact students' progress.	Collaborate with colleagues across the campus on activities that further the mission.

Industry Context, as shown in Table 7.5, comprises the subcomponent areas of news and events, sector knowledge, functional knowledge, and student trends. Professionals who have industry context are aware of activities that take place in external settings, particularly at other institutions, and can offer perspectives that are informed by knowledge of broader national trends.

Table 7.6 displays the Strategy and Planning subcomponents, which are role alignment, project management, resource allocation, and progress monitoring. These areas are primarily related to the ability to develop a sequence of activities and determine the timing and investments necessary to complete each step of a process.

Interpreting Results

The self-assessment exercise should illuminate that every professional has a role in creating and sustaining a climate of data use on campus. With regard to specific combinations of data identity components and related abilities, there are 15 different combinations of two data identity components. These combinations are listed as follows and displayed in Table 7.7 in no particular order.

1. Curiosity and Inquiry + Research and Analysis
2. Curiosity and Inquiry + Communication and Consultation
3. Curiosity and Inquiry + Campus Context
4. Curiosity and Inquiry + Industry Context
5. Curiosity and Inquiry + Strategy and Planning
6. Research and Analysis + Communication and Consultation
7. Research and Analysis + Campus Context
8. Research and Analysis + Industry Context
9. Research and Analysis + Strategy and Planning
10. Communication and Consultation + Campus Context
11. Communication and Consultation + Industry Context
12. Communication and Consultation + Strategy and Planning
13. Campus Context + Industry Context
14. Campus Context + Strategy and Planning
15. Industry Context + Strategy and Planning

These two-component combinations highlight opportunities for professionals to contribute specific strengths to a collaborative effort. As an example, five different two-component combinations are described as personas that a

TABLE 7.5

Data Identity Self-Assessment Component—Industry Context

Industry Context – Knowledge of Current Issues and Trends in Higher Education

Subcomponent Areas	Emerging Ability	Developing Ability	Strong Ability
News and Events Skill: *Following recent developments that impact the majority of campuses across the country*	Read articles from national newspapers, research and policy organizations, and other sources.	Attend or present at events that focus on current higher education topics.	Summarize themes of current national issues to inform office or department work.
Sector Knowledge Skill: *Understanding topics related to most institutions of the same type (examples: two-year, four-year, public, private)*	Identify peer institutions and review information from the fact book and other publicly available resources.	Review reports, briefs, and other resources that provide benchmarking information about other campuses in the sector.	Summarize themes of current sector issues to inform office or department work.
Functional Knowledge Skill: *Understanding topics related to a department on most campuses (examples: business office, student affairs, academic affairs)*	Converse with a professional from another campus about how the function operates at their institution.	Review reports, briefs, and other resources from national associations or other organizations focused on the campus function.	Engage with colleagues to assess how office or department practices compare to national standards or metrics.
Student Trends Skill: *Understanding various national characteristics and themes related to college students and their progress*	Review documentaries, reports, presentations, interviews, student reflections, and other sources that describe students' college experiences.	Collaborate with colleagues in the office or department to compare national student trends to the campus population.	Analyze national datasets to compare current student trends to national student outcomes.

TABLE 7.6

Data Identity Self-Assessment Component—Strategy and Planning

Strategy and Planning – The Ability to Select and Execute a Course of Action

Subcomponent Areas	Emerging Ability	Developing Ability	Strong Ability
Role Alignment *Skill: Selecting the appropriate people to engage in work together*	Connect each project task to a person with related experience.	Provide guidance or coaching to individuals who need assistance to complete specific tasks.	Form groups, as needed, of professionals who have similar abilities to increase project scale.
Project Management *Skill: Determining the order and time in which activities will be conducted*	Prepare a project work plan and timeline.	Select the processes by which the project activities will be completed.	Realign or reprioritize project activities across all areas of work as needed.
Resource Allocation *Skill: Deciding the appropriate amount of personnel and financial investment for a project or activity*	Identify gaps between needed project resources and those that are available.	Prepare a budget for all project expenses.	Analyze the return on the time, personnel, and financial investments for the project.
Progress Monitoring *Skill: Evaluating the extent to which a project reached the target outcome*	Determine project scope, goals, and primary objectives.	Identify a set of potential project risks and options for managing each.	Select a set of metrics by which outcomes will be measured.

TABLE 7.7

15 Two-Component Combinations of Data Identity

	Curiosity and Inquiry	Research and Analysis	Communication and Consultation	Campus Context	Industry Context	Strategy and Planning
Curiosity and Inquiry		1	2	3 Ex1	4	5
Research and Analysis	1		6 Ex2	7	8	9
Communication and Consultation	2	6		10	11	12
Campus Context	3	7	10 Ex3		13	14
Industry Context	4	8	11	13 Ex4		15
Strategy and Planning	5	9	12	14	15 Ex5	

higher education professional may have in relation to specific roles. Those five example roles are: connector; curator; recruiter; trend observer; and mission monitor. The following personas do not reflect exact levels of ability for each component area but instead focus on the strengths of the five different two-component combinations.

Persona Example 1: The Connector—Curiosity and Inquiry + Campus Context

Professionals who have a combination of Curiosity and Inquiry and Campus Context may be comfortable in the role of a connector. This persona has a natural ability to network with colleagues and identify similarities across emerging issues. For example, someone with this combination could find it easy to connect stakeholder impact to a specific program or initiative, which would help explain why the effort is important and to whom. In essence, the connector has the ability to bring current issues and the people who care about those issues together.

Persona Example 2: The Curator—Research and Analysis + Communication and Consultation

Professionals who have a combination of Research and Analysis and Communication and Consultation could have the role of a curator. This persona is adept at not only finding the most relevant pieces of information to share in a discussion but delivering it in ways that are easy for colleagues to understand. For example, a curator could combine the ability to compute data with skill at interpreting the results for a variety of audiences. This pair of abilities is helpful to any data-informed project.

Persona Example 3: The Recruiter—Communication and Consultation + Campus Context

Those who have the combination of Communication and Consultation and Campus Context could have the role of a recruiter. The recruiter persona is one that is especially skilled at brokering support from colleagues and soliciting their help with projects. Someone in this role typically has a deep understanding of various campus issues and can easily explain the nuance of why certain trends are worth colleagues' attention. That pair of abilities is excellent for data-informed projects that directly connect to the campus mission.

Persona Example 4: The Trend Observer—Campus Context + Industry Context

A professional who has the combination of Campus Context and Industry Context would be good in a role of trend observer. A trend observer is someone who provides perspectives about how campus activities compare to those of other institutions. For example, a person who has this pair of abilities and is part of a project team that is examining transfer student issues could have knowledge of state or national developments about transfer students across the United States. The trend observer's input is especially valuable to projects that involve using data to execute a new strategy.

Persona Example 5: The Mission Monitor—Strategy and Planning + Campus Context

Those who have a combination of Strategy and Planning and Campus Context could have the role of mission monitor. The mission monitor is skilled at developing action plans that are aligned with the institution's primary objectives. For example, this persona could leverage knowledge of the campus strategic plan in discussions about allocating resources for a project. Such a combination of abilities would help the professional not only determine which resources are most valuable to a project but also speculate how those resources, if invested, could help advance the institution's primary goals.

Additional Considerations

This discussion of how the six data identity components can help professionals in their daily work could prompt one to consider how to intentionally align the data identity framework with job responsibilities. One may be inclined to approach this idea with a focus on how a professional's data identity connects to specific job duties. An assumption might be that certain data identity components require more skill depending on one's level of responsibility. For example, it would be easy to assume that a professional in a cabinet-level position will perform work related to strategy and planning at a high level. However, someone who is in a coordinator role but responsible for an entire scope of work for a project may also exhibit more skill in the same area. As mentioned earlier, the components can be highly contextual in that one's experiences and related abilities can vary by institution, function, and specific job.

Those who are responsible for hiring new colleagues or adjusting existing positions could find the data identity components useful when drafting job descriptions. For example, a crosswalk of the data identity framework and current job descriptions will likely reveal several campus positions that require at least a few data identity components. While positions range in level of seniority, many are similar with regard to the types of broad skills required, such as critical thinking, communication, and problem solving, which underscores the need for all professionals to have a variety of data-related abilities. Appendix B provides four position advertisements that contain skills and abilities that connect to data identity framework components.

Conclusion

 El Hakim and Lowe (2020) argue that institutions need to be a safe space where people can speak openly, collaborate equally, suggest freely, critique constructively, and share generously. The process of reflecting on one's natural tendencies, abilities, and interests can provide a good foundation upon which to engage with colleagues. In the following quote, Mitchell Colver from Utah State University (personal communication, January 17, 2020) describes how sharing information can help professionals be successful:

> I teach a class called "Becoming an Educated Consumer of Research" and I teach that research is just a really formalized way of the information gathering process and it's built to help mitigate biases. The point of research, at its core, is to kind of go "here's something interesting" and then share it with other people. So, if I'm thinking about skillsets, I think curiosity is really key. Second, you actually have to care and ask questions. Third, I think some kind of tracing is really essential. We call it measurement but it's like making a record or keeping notes. It's a willingness to share and test your conclusions or assumptions against other people's experiences. So, those three, I would say, are a trifecta for being successful.

Upon completing the data identity self-assessment, professionals could review their results together with a goal of finding opportunities to combine their respective strengths. One exercise is to create additional personas for the remaining 10 identity pairings. Such efforts to proactively communicate help create and sustain a campus climate that is ripe for more data-informed practices. For example, when asked for advice to professionals for how to stay motivated when doing data-related work, Caroline Maulana at the University of South Carolina (USC; personal communication,

December 20, 2019) provided the following response, which highlights the value of seeking opportunities to engage with others:

> Create a team of people who motivate you. At UofSC, I have created an analytics community of practice that is inclusive of staff, faculty, as well as students. I compose a monthly newsletter featuring various topics on analytics and I include related free events taking place in the area. I also try to not just highlight the technical aspects of reporting, as the whole point of the community is to build some excitement around data and analytics.

The data identity self-assessment exercise can help professionals identify the actions they need to take now and in the future. Professionals who interpret their results and develop learning plans will be better prepared for an ever-changing higher education landscape. The next chapter focuses on the future of data use in higher education and primary considerations for those who intend to increase their capacity to make data-informed decisions in the years ahead.

8

THE FUTURE OF DATA
USE ON CAMPUS:
INTERSECTIONS OF
TECHNOLOGY AND HUMAN
DECISION-MAKING

Technology and AI are not going to slow down so we have to catch up with it. I feel that in the next five to ten years, folks will be able to mesh the AI piece with the need for efficiencies. Offices and people that start becoming tighter and leaner are going to be the ones who are still standing. But, I will also say that there's an importance of human connection that AI cannot replace. So, what are we doing to prepare ourselves to speak to the value of human connection while not negating the fact that there are some things that AI can replace?

—Khalilah Doss, University of Southern Indiana

This quote (K. Doss, personal communication, January 17, 2020) underscores the focus of this chapter, which is the intersection of technology and human decision-making. Chapter 1 references artificial intelligence, predictive modeling, and algorithms, all of which are commonplace terms in campus data conversations today. Technology enables campuses to automate processes, integrate systems, and increase connections among professionals in physical and virtual spaces. However, technology cannot replace human touch nor can it fully interpret various campus contexts. It is for these reasons that over the next several years, professionals will need to not only understand where and when to leverage technology but how to do so while maximizing their unique and irreplaceable human skillsets.

This chapter weaves the discussion of data, technology, and human decision-making by offering eight predictions about the future of data use on college campuses, as reflective of background interviews, research, and national trends. When asked about the future of data use on campus, professionals mentioned several expected topics such as a continued need for stewardship and governance, the impact of predictive modeling, and shifting roles and responsibilities. Those themes as well as several others are covered in the following predictions.

Prediction 1: Technology and Data Will Help Professionals Provide Better Experiences for Students

Data-informed decision-making requires a combination of individual commitments to using information to make improvements. The process is often clear in concept but difficult in practice, as professionals may have varying interpretations of data and different perspectives regarding what changes are needed. The work to use data to improve myriad student experiences will sometimes be challenging and uncomfortable. However, in the following quote, Melissa Ann Brown from the University of Tennessee, Knoxville (personal communication, December 12, 2019) describes why professionals should welcome the opportunity:

> Data is intended to provide you with the information that helps you do better for students. So, if the data reveals that your practices are not best, be excited about that because now you know you need to make changes to impact that student experience for the better. We have to get out of our feelings about what data says and put action and practice to what we've learned.

Despite the difficulty of finding an ideal workflow, institutions will continue to use data to deliver efficient instruction, programs, and services. As one considers the cost of these resources, a goal of efficiency will lead many professionals to reduce expenditures. It is expected that institutions will focus on cost reduction as a result of industry changes, unexpected economic downturns, and other factors. But, in situations that are less unpredictable, professionals will not just use data to select resources to reduce or eliminate but also to maximize existing resources. Gail DiSabatino at the University of Massachusetts Boston (personal communication, January 2, 2020) describes that approach in the following quote:

> We have this proliferation in higher education of so many things trying to be all things to all people. I think that's part of the reason it has become so

costly but not the sole reason. I think as we continue to increase our use of data, we'll see opportunities for closing things down because they're inefficient. We'll take limited resources and redirect them into what data is telling us is being effective and useful. I think that's already starting and I think that's going to become much more of a trend over the next five years.

Prediction 2: Professionals Will Use Data to Provide Holistic Learning Experiences

As mentioned in chapter 5, more institutions are intentionally connecting classroom-based and cocurricular experiences to give students more integrated learning opportunities. Improved learning environments could certainly influence the traditional markers of student success, which are typically the rates at which students persist, are retained, and graduate. While these indicators are worth tracking, research from Busteed (2017) suggests that more success indicators are needed, as 51% of adults said they would change at least one aspect of their college education experience.

Parnell (2018) describes the need for campuses to expand their definition of student success to include the following four holistic, present, and future-focused indicators which supplement traditional metrics:

- A successful student knows when and how to adapt to or attempt to change their environment.
- A successful student understands their own needs and the needs of others and knows how to balance competing individual and community priorities.
- A successful student knows how to manage resources, both those for which they are individually responsible and those they share responsibility for with others.
- A successful student realizes their unique contributions to the world and is prepared to leverage their abilities to improve the conditions around them.

Though indicators such as these are harder to measure and vary by student, college experiences that provide these and other types of holistic learning will benefit students now and in the years to come. Professionals who gather information regarding students' perspectives and sentiments about college can leverage the Campus Context component of their data identity to monitor the extent to which learning is happening everywhere.

Prediction 3: Professionals Will Use More Data to Prioritize College Affordability and Career Readiness

Gagliardi and Wellman (2015) found that 76% of campus IR offices reported that the degree to which their studies positively impact the reduction of students' cost of attendance was low or very low. Parnell et al. (2018) examined how campuses are prioritizing data studies and found that 46% of campuses reported not conducting studies about students' ability to afford higher education. The cost of college will likely continue to increase, and students' ability to cover the cost will be a factor in their ability to complete a credential. As institutions strive to develop even more precise projections of student enrollment, professionals across the campus should expect to use data and information to better understand students' financial capability.

For many students, the primary reason for attending college is to attain skills that can prepare them for a job. However, Selingo (2016) argues that employers do not want to hire new college graduates who have not worked or interned anywhere. Career services professionals are helping students prepare for work with a variety of practices and resources such as mock interviews and career advising. While dedicated career services offices typically have the majority of these responsibilities, research suggests that career readiness will be a focus of many other campus functions as well, as the National Association of Colleges and Employers (NACE; 2019) reports that nearly seven of eight career services offices work with academic departments to help students obtain internships. As some institutions, especially those in the public sector, continue to be evaluated on the rates at which graduates attain jobs, pressure will mount for professionals to use data to identify the best ways to give students the most career preparation possible.

Prediction 4: Institutions Will Increase Their Use of Data to Address Accountability

As mentioned in chapter 4, the emphasis on outcomes will continue to push institutions to use data to show that programs are successful and students are reaching expected milestones. Similar to the reference to career readiness in the previous prediction, in the following quote Kimberly Lowry from Lone Star College (personal communication, January 17, 2020) describes how data will be an integral part of explaining the value of college now and in the future:

> I think more and more we're going to have to demonstrate what we are doing and what type of outcomes we're producing. I think that's related to

stewardship because of finances but also students. At the end of the day, if the value of college is what we know it to be, how can we demonstrate through data that people are getting jobs, increasing their living wage, and that communities are better?

It does nothing for me to have 5,000 students here if none are completing, none are getting jobs, and none are able to contribute to society. So I think, for me, in five years we should know much more about who we serve, what we're doing, and if it's working. If it's not, we should be able to document and articulate how we've assessed that and are making changes to bring about these ultimate goals.

In addition to being accountable to outside entities, the future of data use on campus will likely involve professionals increasing their accountability to each other. A widespread and positive climate for data use will be more important than ever, as colleagues share both successes and missteps and support each other in pursuing the campus mission. Colleagues who welcome vulnerability, iterative planning, and incremental progress will be well-positioned to use data to address the various accountability measures that lie ahead.

Prediction 5: The Safeguarding of Students' Data Will Remain a Challenge for Some Colleges

Kurzweil and Stevens (2018) state that it is time for a forward-focused discussion of how to define ethical information practice in academia. Such a focus will undoubtedly have to address issues related to the effective management of students' information. Jon Jon Federic S. Chua from Rockland Community College describes the importance of data privacy in the following short reflection (personal communication, December 16, 2019): "With the ever-changing educational background and innovation, I think data privacy has to be increased. We have to have more security and more safeguards so the institution will not be hacked."

Although campuses are required to protect students' data, it is likely that in some instances, new methods of gathering student-related information will emerge faster than professionals can develop processes. As a result, some institutions will continue to have difficulty resolving data privacy issues. For example, practices such as location tracking help professionals monitor students' specific behaviors and highlight a need to prevent inappropriate use of the information. In the future, institutions will continue to prepare for unexpected data breaches, updated regulations regarding access, and other data protection issues. Professionals can help with those efforts by using the

Curiosity and Inquiry portion of their data identity to determine what student information is most needed and how to ensure it is not mishandled.

Prediction 6: Data Will Continue to Illuminate Inequities Throughout All Sectors of Higher Education

Education in the United States has struggled with inequities for decades. In the K–12 sector, schools are experiencing vastly different student outcomes that unfortunately show wide disparities for students across various racial, ethnic, and income backgrounds. Those trends have permeated higher education as well, as not only do individual campuses have wide variances in student outcomes, but outcome disparities remain across the entire field as a whole. There are good reasons for examining demographic differences, and Grawe (2018) argues that with regard to recruitment pools, analyzing subsets of the population according to geography, race, or ethnicity is a step in the right direction.

As institutions prepare for more diverse learner populations to apply in the years ahead, professionals have an opportunity to use data to examine variations in how student groups are experiencing college. In the following quote, Kenyon Bonner from the University of Pittsburgh (personal communication, January 17, 2020) describes how institutions can use their data to identify and address inequitable practices and outcomes:

> Using data to address equity issues in higher education is going to be critical. I think historically, we've used data in aggregate and looking at the big picture. I think you need to look at it from an equity lens and begin to disaggregate the data in all types of ways to really understand the various populations and how they're experiencing college whether it is access and affordability, sense of belonging, satisfaction, or academic performance.
>
> I think that's going to be critical but you need people on your campus who have that lens to look deeper than the aggregate. So, I think that's going to be really important for higher education and that's going to help us if there is a willingness to dismantle the inequality that's embedded in the structure of higher education.

It is common for institutions to prioritize using data to check for equitable outcomes across student populations. For example, professionals likely analyze information to determine the extent to which underserved populations are keeping pace academically and financially. While this is a focus that certainly needs to continue, professionals should also use data to ensure that they are not creating new types of inequities. In addition to using data to examine outcomes, the future will require institutions to also monitor processes. For example, a decision to move an entire degree program or a cocurricular experience to an online format could impact students differently, depending on their abilities or available resources. Although educational inequities will likely persist in the future, professionals who use data to discover the nuances of the issue will help it remain a campus priority.

Prediction 7: Students Will Become Consumers and Stewards of Data

Of the many factors that influence students' ability to complete a degree, their financial position, level of engagement with the campus, and academic progress are three of the leading indicators. Just as consumers become more accustomed to having tools that help track such things as daily spending and budgeting, the habit of proactively using data to check one's progress will likely spread into higher education. For example, research suggests that the earlier students can learn about financial aid the better, as Carnevale and Smith (2018) argue that integrating financial aid into the curriculum rather than offering an occasional workshop can help normalize students' financial understanding at an early age. Students who are making tough financial decisions will start to expect more information about their options. As a result, future campus data discussions will include students as consumers of their own information.

One point of interest for students will be visualizations of their level of campus engagement. In the future, students will be more attuned to how they can show, with data, the skills and competencies they are acquiring. The timing for this is good, as more institutions are using comprehensive learner records that can both store and display information about students' connection to the campus. For example, Eynon and Gambino (2018) describe the e-Portfolio as a practice that, if done well, supports reflection, integration, and deep learning and helps students make connections. These connections will involve students engaging with campus professionals to gather data and artifacts for their official engagement records. As students ask more focused questions about how their involvement with the campus can help them succeed, professionals can leverage the Communication and Consultation component of their data identity to help them interpret their progress.

In the next few years, students will also consume more information about their academic progress. As institutions become more sophisticated in their use of predictive modeling, conversations between professionals and students will shift to focus on specific details and actions that students can take. For example, in the following quote Steve Wisniewski from the University of Pittsburgh (personal communication, December 20, 2019) describes a kind of academic data that students will request in the future:

> I think there's going to be a lot more information pushed directly to students on their progress. Not only from the global perspective of things like time to graduation, but feedback on where they stand in courses, relative to their peers and those who have taken the course in the past. This type of interaction is common with the current generation of students who have grown up in a world where analytics are used to push information to them on a daily basis.

Prediction 8: Artificial Intelligence Will Not Replace Human Decision-Making

The debate of whether artificial intelligence will create such efficiencies and levels of precision that professionals will not be as needed is one that will continue in the future. However, rather than question whether technology will make some campus roles obsolete, a better focus is on how technology can lead to enhanced and new ways of working. While predictive models help identify students who could benefit from more proactive resources, the actual delivery is in many instances completed by a person. In a similar comparison, a model may prescribe a specific action that should be taken, but professionals are experts about how the process should occur within campus contexts. For example, one of the many invaluable professional interactions with students is the advising process. In the following quote, Mark Cooper from the University of South Carolina (personal communication, January 16, 2020) describes how predictive modeling could lead students to an ideal major:

> When students pick classes and majors, they're often doing that based on very limited information. Most students coming out of high school may have no clue what two-thirds of the possible majors on their campus are and this all skews demographically. What I know about higher education suggests that restricting students' choice is not going to be a winner. It's going to produce demoralized students. So, we need predictive analytics that helps students, based on some inputs, figure out majors that they might not have even thought would have been successful for them.

Advisers may leverage predictive modeling to help narrow a set of options for students but will still have the opportunity to talk with them about their educational goals and desires. It is expected that some professionals will find the task of supplementing their work with artificial intelligence both counterintuitive and challenging. However, data-informed decision-making is still the goal and though roles and responsibilities may change, humans will be needed to do things that cannot be replicated by machines.

Conclusion

Whether professionals' future plans relate to improving students' experiences, addressing inequities, or managing the resources for which they are held accountable, technology will be essential to campuses in the years ahead. The eight predictions and related interview quotes and research suggest that data and technology will continue to help institutions identify efficient options and new solutions. However, neither will replace the human touch that makes higher education professionals' work so valuable. In instances when data-informed discussions of return on investment, scenario planning, and revenue forecasting reveal inefficiencies, it will be critical for professionals to not silo roles and responsibilities but instead work more closely together. The next chapter concludes this book with a summary of themes and an emphasis on how every college professional will continue to be a data person in the future.

CONCLUSION

I think for us, the thing that's the most challenging is to look at student progression post-graduation. That requires being able to follow up with every student who graduates once they get into their profession three to five years out. It would be to ask them "What is it about what you learned in undergrad that most impacted your work life?" I'm a full story person. I like to see things from the beginning to the end and it doesn't stop once they leave undergrad. It would be really time-consuming and resource-heavy but I would love to follow all students at least three to five years out.

—Elijah Cameron, Georgia Institute of Technology

For those who desire to influence change on their campus, there are several indicators that this a good time to strive for making data-informed decisions. Institutions are making visible commitments to scalable outcomes, and divisions, departments, and units are acknowledging the importance of holistic approaches to serving students. These conditions are perfect for professionals who have aspirations such as those described in the previous quote (E. Cameron, personal communication, January 14, 2020), as curiosity, inquiry, and intentionality will be commonplace now and in the future. This chapter concludes the discussion of data use on college campuses with a recap of four key themes throughout the book: student experiences; understanding the data identity framework; practical uses of data; and the importance of collaboration.

Student Experiences

Many institutions across the United States assert that student success is a priority. Campuses are now displaying that commitment in several ways: positions, programs, departments, metrics, and mission. Each of these areas, though approached in different ways, displays the importance of students being the focal point for campus activities. Positions such as director of student success are responsible for coordinating campus-wide student success initiatives and summits. Some campuses have an office of student success or student success center, which organizes a variety of ongoing support services. As a result, campuses are also monitoring metrics related to students' progress and performance. Institutions typically frame these and other efforts as part of their mission and a strategic dedication to student success.

Students' experiences in college, when developed well and delivered optimally, provide the foundation for their longer-term success. Chapter 6 addressed specific outcomes of integrated learning and argued that students' development of evergreen abilities should be a goal for every institution. Additional areas such as health and well-being, academic progression, and financial capability are also relevant to students' progress. Some of these were included in chapter 6, which provided a list of examples for professionals to consider. In the following quote, Ashari James from Rockland Community College describes a consistent use of data for the purpose of assessing student experiences (personal communication, November 18, 2019):

> With regard to my decision-making, I go about 80 to 85 percent off data. I have to assess who utilizes services, who didn't utilize services, and how it impacted the students. I also have to determine some steps we need to take, who I need to contact, and my target audience. So, for my decisions in the functions that I have to oversee, I utilize data.

In their report on defining student success data, the Higher Learning Commission (2018) states that student success is not just about getting students to and through college, but about redesigning institutions to support students in the complex interplay of their lived experience. It may be undeniable that such redesign is overdue, as inequities among students remain. Institutions that are willing to pursue myriad changes may still struggle with the process of doing so, especially with regard to the timing of certain interventions, programs, and initiatives. Professionals can leverage the Curiosity and Inquiry part of their identity to include students in their deliberations about how to improve campus experiences. As mentioned in the previous chapter, students will likely become consumers and stewards of data, and by gathering students' perceptions of what successful experiences entail, professionals can better align resources with students' needs.

Understanding the Data Identity Framework

Two primary purposes of this book were to introduce the concept of a data identity and show professionals how to leverage their identity to make informed decisions. The data identity framework in chapter 2 presented six areas in which every higher education professional, regardless of their role or responsibility, should have experience. Chapter 7 provided descriptions of the 24 subcomponents of one's data identity and examples of how certain combinations can reveal various personas. The book is designed to motivate professionals to both understand their identity and welcome the opportunity to use it when working with others. The following quote from Emily Feuer at the University at Albany is a great example of how one's understanding of their strengths and areas for improvement can help in a collaborative setting (personal communication, December 18, 2019):

> I think the biggest contributor to my success is definitely other professionals. My predecessor really helped me out and IR helps me all the time. I think the one thing that I've learned is that you have to be willing to say you don't know or that you're not feeling confident about something. Every time I've said one of those things, someone has always jumped in and helped me out.

Perhaps the most promising part of the previous quote is that it describes how professionals can learn from each other. Those who use the self-assessment exercise included in chapter 7 should do so with an individual goal of continuous improvement rather than finite measurement of abilities. The assessment is a guide to help professionals discover the valuable skills they possess and the underutilized competencies they can develop. Chapter 3 suggested reports and other resources for those who are at emerging, developing, or strong levels of ability in the six data identity areas.

In addition to understanding the individual benefits of the self-assessment, it is important to consider how the exercise can be used for planning. For example, in instances when colleagues realize that they have opposite strengths, the self-assessment should not be used for the purpose of ranking positions or prioritizing the contributions of staff in certain roles. A more appropriate use of the self-assessment is to develop a strategy that acknowledges how professionals with varying abilities and ability levels can participate in a project.

Practical Uses of Data

As mentioned in the introduction, this book is intentionally titled *You Are a Data Person: Strategies for Using Analytics on Campus* to entice professionals across higher education to recognize the breadth of their capacity to make data-informed decisions. The opening proclamation that everyone can find a use for data in their daily work signals that the audience for this book is every person who works at an institution, rather than only those who have dedicated roles such as data scientist or analyst. Chapter 3 provided five rules for individuals to remember as they apply their data identity and chapter 4 followed with a discussion of the intersection of needs, processes, and outcomes. The introduction announced that now is a pivotal time for campuses to use data, and the following quote from Carolyn Livingston at Carleton College describes how doing so could improve public perceptions of why it is a priority (personal communication, January 13, 2020).

> I think the future will bring some skepticism about data. I think that we have done a good job of collecting data but we haven't shared with people how we're using it or the impact or difference that it has made. It's one thing for our students to complete a survey on food service, but if they don't see the impact of what they shared, we're going to get a bunch of jaded people who aren't confident in our data gathering process. I think collecting of data and assessment-driven processes is kind of like the standard right now. But, the high ground is using it.

Chapter 5 provided practical examples of how various functions, departments, and divisions can use data to improve program and service delivery. As professionals attempt to balance present and future issues, periodic audits of processes will be essential. For example, if an unexpected event results in disruption of business operations, campuses should be prepared to execute a planned course of action. By proactively determining which business practices are most and least susceptible to failing amid major changes, professionals can organize their systems and structures to respond accordingly.

As technology advances continue in the future, campuses will also continue to navigate the balance between artificial intelligence and human decision-making. The book referenced institutions' adoption of predictive models to identify students who may need additional support. While the efficiencies that can result from using artificial intelligence could prompt some professionals to be concerned about machines replacing humans in certain roles, chapter 8 provided a rationale for a successful coexistence of human and machine contributions. Singer (2019) states that artificial intelligence presents a profound potential to address some of higher education's most vexing challenges and adds that the focus should be on preserving sufficient control over its influence rather than whether or not to embrace its potential. Professionals who do so will learn to combine it with their inherent skillsets even more effectively.

Importance of Collaboration

Although the self-assessment exercise is designed to help professionals understand their individual abilities, this book emphasizes the significance of teamwork. Ward-Roof and Hands (2016) state that professionals have admirable skillsets and are able to accomplish a great deal on their own but joining with others creates a more comprehensive response, program, or service. This is certainly true with regard to collaborative uses of data, and in the following quote, Mykel Beorchia at Utah State University describes how removing silos helps professionals work together in a better way (personal communication, February 4, 2020):

> In my experiences, the data has helped us break down the institutional silos that we often work in. Having the right conversations about the data allows our shared initiatives to gain momentum throughout the institution. So, without having rich conversations about data, it is really easy for us to work in silos. The conversations centered on the data lead us to buying into the truths that we're seeing through the data and taking collaborative action on improving student success. The right conversations allow us to be even more effective and we continue to knock down the vacuums that we've been working in.

As mentioned in the introduction, the most ideal climate for successful data work is one that promotes open communication, supportive sharing of progress and results, and ongoing collaboration. During the background interviews for the book, individuals shared a source of professional development that greatly helped them understand data. While a few professionals mentioned specific academic courses, training sessions, or books, the majority said their greatest learning came from working with a colleague. One especially important part of collaboration is language. Chapter 1 defined several commonly used terms, and the descriptions of the Curiosity and Inquiry component of the data identity framework stress the value of asking clear questions. Colleagues who can understand each other will find the process of addressing tough issues a bit smoother.

A good example of how colleagues across functional areas can partner is the joint paper released by the Association for Institutional Research, National Association of College and University Business Officers (NACUBO), and EDUCAUSE, the leading associations for institutional researchers, business officers, and information technology professionals respectively. The three membership organizations released *A Joint Statement on Analytics*, which offers six guiding principles for effective and sustained use of data. These principles, which are written as succinct statements, are both a call to action and a visible prompt for professionals to work together. One statement simply states that analytics is a team sport and encourages campuses to build their dream team (NACUBO et al., 2019).

Background interviews for the book also focused on the extent to which professionals perceived their campus climate for data use as positive.

Themes from their responses indicate that the climate is often better when colleagues have opportunities to share what they know and to be honest about what they do not know. The climate is typically challenging when data are used in ways that promote control, power, or competition. Shrinking budgets, increased accountability, and shifting priorities can create environments in which professionals may feel pressured to show, with data and information, that their efforts have been successful. In such instances, it is especially important for professionals to recall the intersection of needs, processes, and outcomes and use data for collaborative conversations.

Closing Thoughts

EDUCAUSE (2020b) states that higher education is always shaping and being shaped by macro trends unfolding in the world surrounding it. As pundits, researchers, scholars, practitioners, politicians, and others continue to discuss and debate the impact of higher education on society, the already widespread use of data on college campuses will be even greater in the years ahead. This book serves to inspire professionals to seek opportunities to make data-informed decisions. The chapters weave together resources, quotes, and examples to show that while the higher education landscape will be as complex in the coming years as it is today, success is not only possible but everyone has something valuable to contribute.

Those who commit to ongoing exploration and understanding of their data identity are poised to face their institution's most difficult challenges. The result will be dynamic cross-functional collaborations and classes of college students who experience the best learning environments their institution can provide. This book has many predictions, but the greatest one of all is that the future of data use in higher education will be bright. That is because the thousands of campuses across the United States are filled with data people, and that includes everyone.

This book arrives at a time when the world is recognizing the many ways in which crises can impact communities at scale. Those who live in the United States, for example, now have visible evidence that racial inequities and injustices remain under-addressed, which directly connects to several systems, including higher education. On a global level, prior to the release of this book, the world experienced the start of COVID-19, a pandemic that has significantly altered the cadence of not just higher education systems but everyday life. As a result, disparities related to income, wealth, health, safety, and other areas are undeniable, and as individuals seek to explain the depth of these conditions, data will be a resource for describing the nuances within each situation.

With regard to higher education, it is obvious that these deep environmental shifts are requiring nearly every institution to deliver instruction, programs, and services in new and unscripted ways and the colloquial phrase "learning on the fly" is more relevant than ever. Chapter 4 explains the intersection of needs, processes, and outcomes, which is especially timely as professionals attempt to reexamine core needs, redesign routine practices, and reevaluate measures of progress. Institutions are now forced to create a new type of campus environment, one that is more attentive to diverse student populations and more flexible to allow swift changes when necessary.

As institutions attempt to describe what a new version of normal business operations will entail, many will rely heavily on data for two important purposes: crisis management and change management. Both of these priorities will be necessary as higher education professionals make critical short- and long-term decisions. Now is the time for everyone who has a college-related role to embrace their data identity and proactively work with colleagues to allocate resources and plan activities that are efficient and sustainable.

In terms of crisis management, professionals will be challenged with using data to identify and manage risks, especially those related to situations that are beyond their control. In previous years, such scenario planning would involve using data to account for disruptions to regular operating procedures that would resume after a break. Such instances as natural disasters are to be expected periodically, and campuses, to some degree, have developed strategies to manage those occurrences. However, the pandemic has illuminated the need for additional and more precise short-term planning for operations that require not just a pause but a pivot from routine practices. For example, in the years ahead, institutions' use of data for such purposes as contact tracing will be commonplace and professionals will need to broaden their understanding of the data privacy regulations mentioned in chapter 1.

In relation to change management, the assertions of this book are especially relevant to institutions that are developing new approaches for aligning personnel with strategic plans. Chapter 7 describes several ways that professionals can use combinations of certain data skills to contribute to projects. As higher education continues to experience the rapid shift to a more blended delivery of in-person and virtual resources, one's understanding of their data-related strengths will be essential. For example, it is likely that higher education job descriptions will change to include more cross-functional responsibilities and more reliance on data that is integrated between multiple sources. While mandatory reporting of key data metrics will remain, the more strategic use of data to predict outcomes and prescribe solutions will be of greater focus. As a result, it will be important for professionals to communicate the most salient parts of their data identity, especially those related to campus context.

One of the most significant ways that institutions can use data to improve their campus in the future is to leverage it to address racial inequities and injustices. As professionals become more willing to both acknowledge the pervasive disparities that exist and work to dismantle the systems and structures from which the problems stem, their use of data will be paramount. While such work will remain hard and complex, the good news is that each campus effort to use data for this purpose creates an opportunity for students to experience the welcoming and affirming environment that they need to thrive. Their likelihood of having a successful college experience will exponentially increase, and that is arguably one of the greatest goals for any data person to strive to achieve.

Supplemental Notes for the Data Identity Self-Assessment Exercise

The self-assessment exercise in chapter 7 is designed to help individuals understand the fullness of their data identity. The 24 additional subcomponents provide greater specificity for the six main component areas. When determining the current level of their ability in each area, one may find that, in some instances, the options are difficult to decipher. This appendix provides supplemental notes to guide professionals' understanding of the nuance in each of the six components. The goal is not absolute prescription or finite measurement of abilities but instead more clarity and framing of one's unique and data-related skills and knowledge. The seven additional points related to self-analysis, investment, and individual experiences are especially relevant as professionals complete the self-assessment exercise:

Self-Analysis

1. The following tables (Tables A.1–A.6) contain 72 actions related to one's data identity. There are certainly more skills than the four listed for each subcomponent as well as more activities for each ability level than the ones listed. The goal of the exercise is to select the 24 options that best describe one's current condition and behaviors. .

2. The subcomponents should not be weighted. For example, in the Communication and Consultation area, delivery type is just as important as interpretation.

Investment

3. Professionals who have an emerging ability will likely engage in certain activities on occasion and at a novice level. Those who have a developing ability will do so more frequently and at a level of some responsibility. Those who have a strong ability will perform certain skills and abilities

on an ongoing basis and, in some instances, at a level that is consistently a model for others to follow.

4. While some levels of ability reflect a greater investment of time, few should require a more significant investment of financial resources. For example, in the Research and Analysis area, those who desire to gain a strong ability related to technical expertise can work on the goal by prioritizing use of existing resources over purchasing new tools.

Individual Experiences

5. There are natural connections between component areas. For example, Curiosity and Inquiry is connected to the Campus Context component in that professionals who understand current campus issues and trends are well-positioned to recognize changes to the pace and flow of campus activities.

6. There are also connections between subcomponent areas. For example, in the Strategy and Planning area, project management, if done well, can help ensure that resource allocations are projected and delivered at optimal levels.

7. When professionals change roles, responsibilities, or institutions, some of their self-selections will also likely change. For example, if a professional who currently works at a private four-year institution accepts a new role at a public four-year institution, their understanding of Industry Context may shift. In a similar example, if a professional who has 15 years of experience at their current institution accepts a new role at a different institution, their understanding of Campus Context will likely shift.

TABLE A.1

Curiosity and Inquiry—The Ability to Formulate and Ask Clear Questions

Subcomponent Areas	Emerging Ability	Developing Ability	Strong Ability
Issue Clarity Skill: Identifying a problem to be addressed	Recognize a change in a campus trend.	Determine the scope and scale of an issue across other areas of the campus.	Articulate how an issue, if unaddressed, will impact various aspects of campus operations.
Question Formation Skill: Determining what information is needed	Gather information that could be relevant to the cause of an issue.	Decipher between information that would be valuable to have versus information that is interesting but less useful.	Transform a list of relevant questions into a set of priority questions to be addressed.
Historical Context Skill: Understanding relevant work that was conducted in the past	Summarize themes from prior reports, briefs, or other resources related to an issue.	Identify results from prior projects that are relevant to a new issue.	Determine whether an issue is significant enough to pursue with a new effort or if it can be addressed with previous solutions.
Stakeholder Impact Skill: Knowing how an issue connects to members of the campus community	Converse with colleagues who have prior experience related to an issue.	Understand why various stakeholders would want an issue resolved.	Determine which stakeholders are most and least affected by an issue.

TABLE A.2
Research and Analysis—The Ability to Select and Use Appropriate Methodologies

Subcomponent Areas	Emerging Ability	Developing Ability	Strong Ability
Methodology Skill: Determining how to address an issue with data and information	Repurpose, with permission, a single data collection resource that is documented as applicable for researching an issue.	Consult with colleagues who have relevant experience to develop a data-informed approach for addressing an issue.	Identify, without need for guidance, the most ideal and reasonable data approach among varying options to address an issue.
Technical Expertise Skill: Using various tools and platforms to study and display data and information	Use resources with little customization to deliver information.	Prepare custom reports and other summaries that are visually appealing and tailored to consumers' specific needs.	Design digital, cloud-based, or online resources that colleagues can use to conduct simple analyses on their own.
Data Integration Skill: Understanding connections among data and information from multiple sources	Gather data from the primary systems used within an office or department.	Refer to various data dictionaries, warehouses, and databases to align data to examine an issue.	Assess weak areas of campus-wide data integration and develop processes for increasing efficiency across systems.
Computation Skill: Using proven research methods to accurately measure outcomes	Prepare simple calculations of data or syntheses of information.	Develop formulas and codes to produce replicable analyses of data and information.	Conduct sophisticated and advanced-level quantitative and qualitative studies of campus data trends.

TABLE A.3

Communication and Consultation—The Ability to Clearly Discuss Findings With Multiple Audiences

Subcomponent Areas	Emerging Ability	Developing Ability	Strong Ability
Delivery Type Skill: Sharing information in a format that is easy to understand	Decipher when a verbal and/or written method is most applicable.	Select the appropriate amount of information to share in a variety of settings.	Explain all information using clear terms and descriptions.
Audience Skill: Determining which information is of most interest to varying individuals	Gather information about individuals' current work portfolios.	Provide practical examples to connect material to individuals' lived experiences.	Translate information to make a topic relevant for a variety of campus professionals.
Interpretation Skill: Explaining myriad concerns and viewpoints in a consistent and clear manner	Identify common interests among multiple people engaged in a discussion.	Connect ideas, perspectives, and questions across a group of colleagues involved in a discussion.	Transform multiple individual viewpoints into a cohesive narrative.
Follow-Up Skill: Identifying opportunities for ongoing collaboration	Maintain a list of ideas and topics for future exploration.	Share project results with new audiences to further refine conclusions.	Provide advice regarding special topics to colleagues across the institution as needs arise.

TABLE A.4

Campus Context—Knowledge of Current Issues and Trends Within the Institution

Subcomponent Areas	Emerging Ability	Developing Ability	Strong Ability
Student Information Skill: Understanding various characteristics of the campus student population and their progress	Review campus fact books or other reports that contain information about student outcomes.	Engage with students who have differing backgrounds to learn about their campus experiences.	Prepare written or verbal syntheses of various student issues over multiple years.
Programs and Initiatives Skill: Knowing how various campus activities are organized and operated	Support activities conducted primarily by one office or unit on campus.	Participate in campus activities in collaboration with colleagues from multiple departments or divisions.	Lead institution-wide activities and, in some instances, manage relationships with external partners.
Strategic Plan Skill: Understanding the most immediate campus priorities	Connect individual job responsibilities to specific objectives in the campus strategic plan.	Align office or department work plans with strategic plan goals and objectives.	Manage activities that contribute to the institution's accreditation or financial stability.
Campus Mission Skill: Working on projects that address the primary purposes for which the institution operates	Identify how individual work addresses students' needs and progress.	Lead office or department projects that directly impact students' progress.	Collaborate with colleagues across the campus on activities that further the mission.

TABLE A.5

Industry Context—Knowledge of Current Issues and Trends in Higher Education

Subcomponent Areas	Emerging Ability	Developing Ability	Strong Ability
News and Events Skill: Following recent developments that impact the majority of campuses across the country	Read articles from national newspapers, research and policy organizations, and other sources.	Attend or present at events that focus on current higher education topics.	Summarize themes of current national issues to inform office or department work.
Sector Knowledge Skill: Understanding topics related to most institutions of the same type (examples: two-year, four-year, public, private)	Identify peer institutions and review information from the fact book and other publicly available resources.	Review reports, briefs, and other resources that provide benchmarking information about other campuses in the sector.	Summarize themes of current sector issues to inform office or department work.
Functional Knowledge Skill: Understanding topics related to a department on most campuses (examples: business office, student affairs, academic affairs)	Converse with a professional from another campus about how the function operates at their institution.	Review reports, briefs, and other resources from national associations or other organizations focused on the campus function.	Engage with colleagues to assess how office or department practices compare to national standards or metrics.
Student Trends Skill: Understanding various national characteristics and themes related to college students and their progress	Review documentaries, reports, presentations, interviews, student reflections, and other sources that describe students' college experiences.	Collaborate with colleagues in the office or department to compare national student trends to the campus population.	Analyze national datasets to compare current student trends to national student outcomes.

TABLE A.6

Strategy and Planning—The Ability to Select and Execute a Course of Action

Subcomponent Areas	Emerging Ability	Developing Ability	Strong Ability
Role Alignment Skill: Selecting the appropriate people to engage in work together	Connect each project task to a person with related experience.	Provide guidance or coaching to individuals who need assistance to complete specific tasks.	Form groups, as needed, of professionals who have similar abilities to increase project scale.
Project Management Skill: Determining the order and time in which activities will be conducted	Prepare a project work plan and timeline.	Select the processes by which the project activities will be completed.	Realign or reprioritize project activities across all areas of work as needed.
Resource Allocation Skill: Deciding the appropriate amount of personnel and financial investment for a project or activity	Identify gaps between needed project resources and those that are available.	Prepare a budget for all project expenses.	Analyze the return on the time, personnel, and financial investments for the project.
Progress Monitoring Skill: Evaluating the extent to which a project reached the target outcome	Determine project scope, goals, and primary objectives.	Identify a set of potential project risks and options for managing each.	Select a set of metrics by which outcomes will be measured.

Mapping Data Identity Components and Sample Higher Education Job Advertisements

The central theme throughout the chapters of the book is that every professional, regardless of their role, has a data identity. As mentioned in chapter 7, one source that supports this theme is job descriptions, because nearly every higher education position has a set of required job responsibilities and necessary skills and abilities. This appendix highlights how four campus positions are connected to various elements of the data identity framework. The following tables display segments of actual job advertisements that were posted online in May 2020. The notations in brackets suggest connections to various components of the data identity framework.

Readers should note the following when reviewing the four positions:

1. Although the positions vary in level of responsibility and are related to different focus areas, several components of the data identity framework can apply to each role. For example, each position appears to connect to the Communication and Consultation component.
2. Connections to the data identity framework are visible in both the listed job responsibilities and the specific and individual knowledge, skills, and abilities that are needed for the roles.
3. The assertions for how each position connects to the data identity framework reflect the author's interpretations of job descriptions only and are not the result of any discussions with hiring managers or other professionals from the institutions. The institutions to which these advertisements connect are omitted as the following tables are intended to be used for illustrative purposes. It is also possible that the positions described as follows may now differ from the actual positions for which individuals have been hired since May 2020.

TABLE B.1

Sample Higher Education Job Advertisement—Clery Compliance Coordinator

Position Title	Sample Job Responsibilities	Sample Skills and Abilities
Clery Compliance Coordinator	Stay abreast of pending and final changes to the Clery Act and other laws or regulations affecting Clery Act provisions and share information with stakeholders **[Industry Context]** Acts as a liaison to campus departments, local law enforcement agencies, and the state police in formulation of data records, facilitation of information sharing, and compilation of annual reports **[Communication and Consultation]** Research, analyze, and monitor developing crime trends, public safety issues, and threats for the campus community and surrounding region **[Research and Analysis and Campus Context]**	Ability to effectively communicate both verbal and written thoughts, ideas, and facts **[Curiosity and Inquiry and Communication and Consultation]** Ability to work collaboratively with others and independently **[Communication and Consultation]**

Source: Chronicle of Higher Education Job Board; Association for Institutional Research Job Board; Higher Ed Jobs.

TABLE B.2
Sample Higher Education Job Advertisement—Data and Research Analyst

Position Title	Sample Job Responsibilities	Sample Skills and Abilities
Data and Research Analyst	Analyze, evaluate, logically interpret, and summarize a wide variety of institutional data to provide timely, relevant, and accurate information to a broad range of internal and external audiences **[Research and Analysis and Communication and Consultation]** Process ad hoc requests and collaborate with data requestors to clarify needs and develop appropriate reporting protocols **[Strategic Planning]** Attend conferences and meetings as assigned **[Industry Context]**	Ability to establish and maintain cooperative and effective working relationships at all levels of the organization **[Communication and Consultation]** Strong critical thinking and interpretive skills to analyze situations, define problems, and develop/implement solutions **[Curiosity and Inquiry and Strategic Planning]** Ability to establish goals, priorities, and timelines and to plan work accordingly **[Strategic Planning]**

Source: Chronicle of Higher Education Job Board; Association for Institutional Research Job Board; Higher Ed Jobs.

TABLE B.3

Sample Higher Education Job Advertisement—Senior Research Scholar

Position Title	Sample Job Responsibilities	Sample Skills and Abilities
Senior Research Scholar	Coordinates with program staff, postdoctoral fellows, consultants, and scholars working in related areas to advance strategic planning, program design, and program evaluation **[Strategic Planning]** Presents research findings and represents the program at academic conferences and educational convenings **[Industry Context]** Assists with the design of interventions based on the science of leadership and character development and best practices in empirical measurement and program evaluation **[Research and Analysis]**	Positively influence colleagues and develop collaborative relationships with a wide range of people **[Communication and Consultation]** Strong analytical and statistical skills with experience using mixed-method (quantitative and qualitative) approaches to empirical research and assessment **[Research and Analysis]**

Source: Chronicle of Higher Education Job Board; Association for Institutional Research Job Board; Higher Ed Jobs.

TABLE B.4

Sample Higher Education Job Advertisement—Director of Advancement Communications

Position Title	Sample Job Responsibilities	Sample Skills and Abilities
Director of Advancement Communications	Curate content within a highly collaborative environment **[Communication and Consultation]** Develop integrated strategies to inform a comprehensive fundraising campaign and contribute new ideas and establish operations that transcend the campaign period **[Strategic Planning and Curiosity and Inquiry]**	Understanding of university advancement best practices related to communications, engagement, cultivation, solicitation, and stewardship **[Industry Context]** Ability to analyze and interpret complex data **[Research and Analysis]** A self-starter who will become immersed in the campus community and beyond to uncover stories about the impact of philanthropy and engagement **[Campus Context]**

Source: Chronicle of Higher Education Job Board; Association for Institutional Research Job Board; Higher Ed Jobs.

REFERENCES

Ajlen, R., Plummer, B., Straub, E., & Zhu, E. (2020). *Motivating students to learn: Transforming courses using a gameful approach.* University of Michigan Center for Research on Teaching and Learning. http://crlt.umich.edu/sites/default/files/resource_files/CRLT_no40.pdf

American Association of Community Colleges. (2020). *Fast facts.* https://www.aacc.nche.edu/wp-content/uploads/2020/03/AACC_Fast_Facts_2020_Final.pdf

Association of American Colleges & Universities. (n.d.-a). *Essential learning outcomes.* https://www.aacu.org/leap/essential-learning-outcomes

Association of American Colleges & Universities. (n.d-b). *VALUE rubrics.* https://www.aacu.org/value-rubrics

Association for Institutional Research. (n.d.-a). *Duties and functions of institutional research.* https://www.airweb.org/ir-data-professional-overview/duties-and-functions-of-institutional-research

Association for Institutional Research. (n.d.-b). *LinkedIn group page.* https://www.linkedin.com/groups/2030443/

Association for Institutional Research. (2020). *Jobs board.* https://www.airweb.org/resources/job-board

Association for the Assessment of Learning in Higher Education. (n.d.). *ASSESS listserv.* https://www.aalhe.org/assess-listserv

Astin, A. W. (1975). *Preventing students from dropping out.* Jossey-Bass.

Board of Governors of the Federal Reserve System. (2019). *Report on the economic well-being of U.S. households in 2018–May 2019.* https://www.federalreserve.gov/publications/2019-economic-well-being-of-us-households-in-2018-student-loans-and-other-education-debt.htm

Bowen, K., Riedel, C., & Essa, A. (2017, April 12). 7 things you should know about artificial intelligence in teaching and learning. *EDUCAUSE.* https://library.educause.edu/resources/2017/4/7-things-you-should-know-about-artificial-intelligence-in-teaching-and-learning

Burd, S., Fishman, R., Keane, L., Habbert, J., Barrett, B., Dancy, K., Nguyen, S., & Williams, B. (2018). *Decoding the cost of college: The case for transparent financial aid award letters.* https://www.newamerica.org/education-policy/policy-papers/decoding-cost-college/

Burke, M., Parnell, A., Wesaw, A., & Kruger, K. (2017). *Predictive analysis of student data: A focus on engagement and behavior.* NASPA–Student Affairs Administrators in Higher Education. https://www.naspa.org/files/dmfile/PREDICTIVE_FULL_4-7-17_DOWNLOAD.pdf

125

Burnside, O., Wesley, A., Wesaw, A., and Parnell, A. (2019). *Employing student success: A comprehensive examination of on-campus student employment.* NASPA–Student Affairs Administrators in Higher Education. https://www.naspa.org/files/dmfile/NASPA_EmploymentStudentSuccess_FINAL_April1_LOWRES_REVISED.pdf

Busteed, B. (2017, June 1). Do you regret your college choices? *Gallup.* https://news.gallup.com/opinion/gallup/211070/regret-college-choices.aspx

California Department of Health Care Services. (n.d.). *Health Insurance Portability & Accountability Act.* https://www.dhcs.ca.gov/formsandpubs/laws/hipaa/Pages/1.00WhatisHIPAA.aspx

Carnevale, A., & Smith, N. (2018). *Balancing work and learning: Implications for low-income students.* Georgetown Center on Education and the Workforce. https://1gyhoq479ufd3yna29x7ubjn-wpengine.netdna-ssl.com/wp-content/uploads/Low-Income-Working-Learners-FR.pdf

Coker, C., & Glynn, J. (2017). *Making college affordable: Providing low-income students with the knowledge and resources needed to pay for college.* Jack Kent Cooke Foundation. https://www.jkcf.org/wp-content/uploads/2018/05/2017-JKCF-Making-College-Affordable-Web.pdf

Colvin, J. W., & Ashman, M. (2010). Roles, risks, and benefits of peer mentoring relationships in higher education. *Mentoring and Tutoring, 18*(2), 121–134. https://doi.org/10.1080/13611261003678879

Conejo, C. (2011, January 1). How to support change management. *The ACA Group.* http://www.theacagroup.com/how-to-support-change-management/

Council for the Advancement of Standards in Higher Education. (2019). *General standards.* https://www.cas.edu/generalstandards

Crutchfield, R., Clark, K., Gamez, S., Green, A., Munson, D., & Stribling, H. (2016). *Serving displaced and food insecure students in the CSU.* California State University. https://presspage-production-content.s3.amazonaws.com/uploads/1487/cohomelessstudy.pdf?10000

D'Amico, M. M., Sublett, C. M., & Bartlett, J. E. (2019). *Preparing the workforce in today's community colleges: Issues and implications for higher education leaders.* American Council on Education. https://www.acenet.edu/Documents/Preparing-the-Workforce-in-Todays-Comty-Colleges.pdf

DeSantis, D., & Glezerman, D. (2013). *College and university business administration: Student financial services.* National Association of College and University Business Officers.

Dontha, R. (2017, February 24). *25 big data terms everyone should know.* Dataconomy. https://dataconomy.com/2017/02/25-big-data-terms/

The Education Trust. (n.d.). *College results online.* http://www.collegeresults.org/default.aspx

EDUCAUSE. (2020a, April 6). *Higher Education Community Vendor Assessment Toolkit.* https://library.educause.edu/resources/2020/4/higher-education-community-vendor-assessment-toolkit

EDUCAUSE. (2020b). *Horizon report: Teaching and learning edition.* https://library. educause.edu/-/media/files/library/2020/3/2020_horizon_report_pdf.pdf?la=en &hash=08A92C17998E8113BCB15DCA7BA1F467F303BA80

El Hakim, Y., & Lowe, T. (2020). Theory and principles underpinning "students engaged in educational developments": SEEDs for the future. In T. Lowe & Y. El Hakim (Eds.), *A Handbook for student engagement in higher education: Theory into practice.* Routledge.

Eynon, B., & Gambino, L. M. (2018). *Catalyst in action: Case studies of high-impact ePortfolio practice.* Stylus.

Fresno State University. (n.d.). *Fresno state student cupboard dashboard.* https:// tableau.fresnostate.edu/views/StudentCupboard/StudentCupboardVisits?if rameSizedToWindow=true&:embed=y&:showAppBanner=false&:display_ count=no&:showVizHome=no

Gagliardi, J. (2018). The analytics revolution in higher education. In J. Gagliardi, A. Parnell, & J. Carpenter-Hubin (Eds.), *The analytics revolution in higher education: Big data, organizational learning, and student success.* Stylus.

Gagliardi, J. S., & Turk, J. M. (2017). *The data-enabled executive.* American Council on Education. https://www.acenet.edu/Documents/The-Data-Enabled-Executive.pdf

Gagliardi, J. S., & Wellman, J. V. (2015). *Meeting demands for improvements in public system institutional research: Assessing and improving the institutional research function in public university systems.* National Association of System Heads. http://nashonline.org/wp-content/uploads/2017/08/Assessing-and-Improving-the-IR-Function-in-Public-University-Systems.pdf

Galanek, J. D., Gierdowski, D. C., & Brooks, D. C. (2018). *ECAR study of undergraduate students and information technology, 2018. Research report.* EDUCAUSE Center for Analysis and Research. https://library.educause.edu/-/media/files/library/2018/10/studentitstudy2018.pdf?la=en&hash=C590C1F6C62B777927 11BFAC1F642254A5618590

Gardner, L. (2019, October 13). Students under surveillance? Data tracking enters a provocative new phase. *Chronicle of Higher Education.* https://www.chronicle. com/article/Students-Under-Surveillance-/247312

Grawe, N. (2018). *Demographics and the demand for higher education.* Johns Hopkins University Press.

Hallett, R. E., & Crutchfield, R. (2017). *Homelessness and housing insecurity in higher education: A trauma-informed approach to research, policy, and practice.* Jossey-Bass.

Henke, N., Levine, J., & McInerney, P. (2018, February 21). You don't have to be a data scientist to fill this must-have analytics role. *Harvard Business Review.* https://hbr.org/2018/02/you-dont-have-to-be-a-data-scientist-to-fill-this-must-have-analytics-role

Higher Learning Commission. (2018). *Defining student success data: Recommendations for changing the conversation.* http://download.hlcommission.org/initiatives/StudentSuccessConversation.pdf

Holman, C. (2018). *Building a better game: A theory of gameful learning and the construction of student personas with agency* (Publication No. 10903042) [Doctoral dissertation, The University of Michigan]. ERIC. ProQuest Dissertations and Theses Global.

Kinzie, J. (2012). High impact practices: Promoting participation for all students. *Diversity and Democracy, 15*(3). https://www.aacu.org/publications-research/periodicals/high-impact-practices-promoting-participation-all-students

Kruger, K., Parnell, A., & Wesaw, A. (2016). *Landscape analysis of emergency aid programs.* NASPA–Student Affairs Administrators in Higher Education. https://www.naspa.org/images/uploads/main/Emergency_Aid_Report.pdf

Kuh, G. D. (1995). The other curriculum: Out-of-class experiences associated with student learning and personal development. *The Journal of Higher Education, 66*(2), 123–155.

Kuh, G. D. (2008). *High-impact educational practices: What they are, who has access to them, and why they matter.* Association of American Colleges and Universities.

Kurzweil, M., & Stevens, M. (2018). *Setting the table: Responsible use of student data in higher education.* EDUCAUSE Review. https://er.educause.edu/articles/2018/5/setting-the-table-responsible-use-of-student-data-in-higher-education

Lane, J. E. (2018). Examining how the analytics revolution matters to higher education policymakers: Data analytics, systemness, and enabling student success. In J. Gagliardi, A. Parnell, & J. Carpenter-Hubin (Eds.), *The analytics revolution in higher education: Big data, organizational learning, and student success.* Stylus.

McNair, T. B., Albertine, S., Cooper, M. A., McDonald, N., & Major, T. (2016). *Becoming a student ready college: A new culture of leadership for student success.* Jossey-Bass.

Merriam-Webster. (n.d.). Algorithm. In *Merriam-Webster.com dictionary.* https://www.merriam-webster.com/dictionary/algorithm

Morse, A., and Woods, K. (2019). *A framework for divisionwide assessments of student learning and institutional effectiveness.* NASPA–Student Affairs Administrators in Higher Education. https://www.naspa.org/images/uploads/main/NASPA_Policy_and_Practice_Issue_5_Divisionwide_Assessment_DOWNLOAD.pdf

National Association of College and University Business Officers, EDUCAUSE, & Association for Institutional Research. (2019). *Analytics can save higher education. Really: A joint statement on analytics.* https://changewithanalytics.com/wp-content/uploads/2020/02/Joint_Analytics_Statement_2020.pdf

National Association of Student Personnel Administrators. (2019). *Employing student success: On-campus student employment self-assessment rubric.* https://www.naspa.org/files/dmfile/NASPA_EmploymentStudentSuccess_Rubric_Compressed.pdf

National Center for Education Statistics (n.d.). *Statutory requirements for reporting IPEDS data.* https://surveys.nces.ed.gov/ipeds/ViewIPEDSStatutoryRequirement.aspx

National Survey of Student Engagement. (2007). *Experiences that matter: Enhancing student learning and success.* Indiana University Center for Postsecondary Research. http://nsse.iub.edu/NSSE_2007_Annual_Report

Northeastern University. (n.d.). *About self-authored integrated learning.* https://sail. northeastern.edu/about

Palmer, I., & Ekowo, M. (2016). *The promise and peril of predictive analytics in higher education: A landscape analysis.* https://www.newamerica.org/education-policy/ policy-papers/promise-and-peril-predictive-analytics-higher-education

Parnell, A. (2018). *It's time for a real definition of student success.* Insights and Outlooks. Higher Learning Advocates. https://higherlearningadvocates.org/2018/08/23/ its-time-for-a-real-definition-of-student-success/

Parnell, A., Jones, D., Wesaw, A., & Brooks, C. C. (2018). *Institutions' use of data and analytics for student success: Results from a national landscape analysis.* https://www. naspa.org/rpi/reports/data-and-analytics-for-studentsuccess

Pusser, B., & Levin, J. (2009). *Reimagining community colleges in the 21st century: A student-centered approach to higher education.* Center for American Progress. https://www.americanprogress.org/wp-content/uploads/issues/2009/12/pdf/ community_colleges_reimagined.pdf

Sarubbi, M. (2019). *Five things student affairs professionals can do to better support foster care alumni on campus.* NASPA–Student Affairs Administrators in Higher Education. https://www.naspa.org/book/five-things-student-affairs-professionals-can-do-to-better-support-foster-care-alumni

SAS. (n.d.). *Predictive analytics: What it is and why it matters.* https://www.sas.com/ en_us/insights/analytics/predictive-analytics.html

Selingo, J. (2016). *There is life after college: What parents and students should know about navigating school to prepare for the jobs of tomorrow.* HarperCollins Publishers.

Singer, F. (2019, January 16). Will higher ed keep AI in check? *Inside Higher Education.* https://www.insidehighered.com/digital-learning/views/2019/01/16/ its-higher-education-keep-ai-check-opinion

Swing, R. L., Jones, D., & Ross, L. E. (2016). *The AIR national survey of institutional research offices.* Association for Institutional Research. http://www.airweb. org/nationalsurvey

Swing, R. L., & Ross, L. E. (2016). *Statement of aspirational practice for institutional research.* Association for Institutional Research. http://www.airweb.org/aspirationalstatement

United States Department of Education. (n.d.-a). *Child care access means parents in school program.* https://www2.ed.gov/programs/campisp/index.html

United States Department of Education. (n.d.-b). *What is FERPA?* https://student-privacy.ed.gov/faq/what-ferpa

United States Department of Education Office of Federal Student Aid. (2020). *Questions and answers: Federal student aid and homeless youth.* https://studentaid. gov/sites/default/files/homeless-youth.pdf

United States Government Accountability Office. (2019). *Report 19-95: Better information could help eligible college students access federal food assistance benefits.* https://www.gao.gov/products/GAO-19-95

University of Central Oklahoma. (n.d.). *Student Transformative Learning Record.* https://www.uco.edu/academic-affairs/stlr/

University of Montana. (n.d.). *Griz family news.* http://www.umt.edu/urelations/ pubs/familynews/default.php

Vasold, K. L., Deere, S. J., & Pivarnik, J. M. (2019). *Benefits of campus recreation: Results of the 2011–2016 recreation and wellness benchmark.* National Intramural and Recreational Sports Association. https://nirsa.net/nirsa/wp-content/uploads/ nirsa-results-of-the-2011-2016-recreation-and-wellness-benchmark-results.pdf

Ward-Roof, J. A., & Hands, A. (2016). Single- versus multiple-AVP structures. In A. Hecht & J. Pina (Eds.), *AVP: Leading from the unique role of associate/ assistant vice president for student affairs.* NASPA–Student Affairs Administrators in Higher Education.

Wesley, A. (2018). *Five things student affairs professionals can do to support adult learners.* NASPA–Student Affairs Administrators in Higher Education. https:// www.naspa.org/images/uploads/main/5Things_ADULTLEARNERS_DOWN-LOAD.pdf

Whitley, S. E., Benson, G., & Wesaw, A. (2018). *First-generation student success: A landscape analysis of programs and services at four-year institutions executive summary.* NASPA–Student Affairs Administrators in Higher Education and Entangled Solutions. https://firstgen.naspa.org/files/NASPA-First-generation-Student-Success-Exec-Summary.pdf

Yeado, J., Haycock, K., Johnstone, R., & Chaplot, P. (2014). *Learning from high-performing and fast-gaining institutions.* The Education Trust. https://edtrust.org/ wp-content/uploads/2013/10/PracticeGuide_0.pdf

ABOUT THE AUTHOR

Amelia Parnell has over 15 years of higher education experience in national, state, and campus-level roles including association management, legislative policy, internal audit, TRIO programs, and graduate-level teaching.

She is currently the vice president for research and policy at NASPA–Student Affairs Administrators in Higher Education, where she leads many of the association's scholarly and advocacy-focused activities. Parnell writes and speaks frequently about topics related to student affairs, college affordability, student learning outcomes, higher education leadership, and institutions' use of data and analytics. Prior to the release of this book, Parnell coedited *The Analytics Revolution in Higher Education: Big Data, Organizational Learning, and Student Success* (Stylus, 2018).

Parnell understands the importance of making data-informed decisions, and she enjoys explaining how professionals can use data to address complex issues. Her ongoing service to the field of higher education includes contributing to several national advisory boards; mentoring students; and hosting her podcast, Speaking of College. Parnell holds a doctorate in higher education from Florida State University and a master's degree and a bachelor's degree in business administration from Florida A&M University.

Faculty Development books from Stylus Publishing

Advancing the Culture of Teaching on Campus
How a Teaching Center Can Make a Difference
Edited by Constance Cook and Matthew Kaplan
Foreword by Lester P. Monts

Faculty Mentoring
A Practical Manual for Mentors, Mentees, Administrators, and Faculty Developers
Susan L. Phillips and Susan T. Dennison
Foreword by Milton D. Cox

Faculty Retirement
Best Practices for Navigating the Transition
Edited by Claire Van Ummersen, Jean McLaughlin and Lauren Duranleau
Foreword by Lotte Bailyn

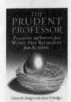

The Prudent Professor
Planning and Saving for a Worry-Free Retirement from Academe
Edwin M. Bridges and Brian D. Bridges

Teaching Across Cultural Strengths
A Guide to Balancing Integrated and Individuated Cultural Frameworks in College Teaching
Alicia Fedelina Chávez and Susan Diana Longerbeam
Foreword by Joseph L. White

Why Students Resist Learning
A Practical Model for Understanding and Helping Students
Edited by Anton O. Tolman and Janine Kremling
Foreword by John Tagg

Graduate and Doctoral Education books from Stylus Publishing

From Diplomas to Doctorates
The Success of Black Women in Higher Education and its Implications for Equal Educational Opportunities for All
Edited by V. Barbara Bush, Crystal Renee Chambers, and Mary Beth Walpole

The Latina/o Pathway to the Ph.D.
Abriendo Caminos
Edited by Jeanett Castellanos, Alberta M. Gloria, and Mark Kamimura
Foreword by Melba Vasquez and Hector Garza

On Becoming a Scholar
Socialization and Development in Doctoral Education
Jay Caulfield
Edited by Susan K. Gardner and Pilar Mendoza
Foreword by Ann E. Austin and Kevin Kruger

Developing Quality Dissertations in the Humanities
A Graduate Student's Guide to Achieving Excellence
Barbara E. Lovitts and Ellen L. Wert

Developing Quality Dissertations in the Sciences
A Graduate Student's Guide to Achieving Excellence
Barbara E. Lovitts and Ellen L. Wert

Developing Quality Dissertations in the Social Sciences
A Graduate Student's Guide to Achieving Excellence
Barbara E. Lovitts and Ellen L. Wert

General Interest books from Stylus Publishing

Are You Smart Enough?
How Colleges' Obsession with Smartness Shortchanges Students
Alexander W. Astin

The New Science of Learning
How to Learn in Harmony With Your Brain
Terry Doyle and Todd D. Zakrajsek
Foreword by Kathleen F. Gabriel

Of Education, Fishbowls, and Rabbit Holes
*Rethinking Teaching and Liberal Education for an
Interconnected World*
Jane Fried with Peter Troiano
Foreword by Dawn R. Person

Managing Your Professional Identity Online
A Guide for Faculty, Staff, and Administrators
Kathryn E. Linder
Foreword by Laura Pasquini

Teach Yourself How to Learn
Strategies You Can Use to Ace Any Course at Any Level
Saundra Yancy McGuire with Stephanie McGuire
Foreword by Mark McDaniel

Pitch Perfect
*Communicating with Traditional and Social Media for
Scholars, Researchers, and Academic Leaders*
William Tyson
Foreword by Robert Zemsky

Job Search/Staff Recruitment & Retention books from Stylus Publishing

The Complete Academic Search Manual
A Systematic Approach to Successful and Inclusive Hiring
Lauren A. Vicker and Harriette J. Royer

Debunking the Myth of Job Fit in Higher Education and Student Affairs
Edited by Brian J. Reece, Vu T. Tran, Elliott N. DeVore and Gabby Porcaro
Foreword by Stephen John Quaye

Establishing the Family-Friendly Campus
Models for Effective Practice
Edited by Jaime Lester and Margaret Sallee

Job Search In Academe
How to Get the Position You Deserve
Dawn M. Formo and Cheryl Reed

The New Talent Acquisition Frontier
Integrating HR and Diversity Strategy in the Private and Public Sectors and Higher Education
Edna Chun and Alvin Evans
Foreword by Andy Brantley and Benjamin D. Reese, Jr.

Search Committees
A Comprehensive Guide to Successful Faculty, Staff, and Administrative Searches
Christopher D. Lee
Foreword by Edna Chun

Professional Development books from Stylus Publishing

Adjunct Faculty Voices
*Cultivating Professional Development and Community at the
Front Lines of Higher Education*
Edited by Roy Fuller, Marie Kendall Brown and
Kimberly Smith
Foreword by Adrianna Kezar

Authoring Your Life
*Developing an INTERNAL VOICE to Navigate Life's
Challenges*
Marcia B. Baxter Magolda
Foreword by Sharon Daloz Parks
Illustrated by Matthew Henry Hall

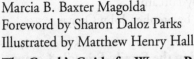

The Coach's Guide for Women Professors
Who Want a Successful Career and a Well-Balanced Life
Rena Seltzer
Foreword by Frances Rosenbluth

Contingent Academic Labor
Evaluating Conditions to Improve Student Outcomes
Daniel B. Davis
Foreword by Adrianna Kezar

Shaping Your Career
A Guide for Early Career Faculty
Don Haviland, Anna M. Ortiz and Laura Henriques
Foreword by Ann E. Austin

What They Didn't Teach You in Graduate School
299 Helpful Hints for Success in Your Academic Career
Paul Gray and David E. Drew
Illustrated by Matthew Henry Hall
Foreword by Laurie Richlin and Steadman Upham

(Continued from preceding page)

Pursuing Quality, Access, and Affordability

A Field Guide to Improving Higher Education

Stephen C. Ehrmann

Foreword by Jillian Kinzie

"In *Pursuing Quality, Access, and Affordability*, Steve Ehrmann advances a compelling narrative on how higher education can be improved. Basing his analysis on six extensive institutional case studies, he outlines how it is possible for institutions to create what he terms "3fold gains" in educational quality, equitable access, and stakeholder affordability. These gains are achieved through Integrative learning-based constellations of mutually supportive educational strategies, organizational foundations, and interactions with the wider world. The book offers a cogent rationale for how such coordinated efforts can enhance quality, access, and affordability on an institutional scale. As higher education prepares for a post-COVID educational landscape much changed by current challenges, now is the time for forward-thinking institutions to imagine this future. And Dr. Ehrmann's careful study, based on actual experiences of institutions that have achieved success in these areas at the core of higher education's mission and purpose, provides an excellent blueprint for success."
—*David Eisler, President, Ferris State University*

The Analytics Revolution in Higher Education

Big Data, Organizational Learning, and Student Success

Edited by Jonathan S. Gagliardi, Amelia Parnell, and Julia Carpenter-Hubin

Foreword by Randy L. Swing

Copublished with AIR and ACE

"Comprised of 13 erudite, impressively informative, and exceptionally thoughtful, thought-provoking articles by experts in the field of big data management and education, *The Analytics Revolution in Higher Education* is an extraordinary and highly recommended addition to both college and university library education and data processing collections and supplemental studies reading lists."—*Midwest Book Review*

From the Foreword:

"*The Analytics Revolution in Higher Education* presents a clear and consistent message that a paradigm shift is taking place around data and analytics in higher education. The case can easily be made for a paradigm shift in data and analytics based on the influx of new technologies and new services provided in data-related higher education decision making. Decision support in the new paradigm includes leadership in questioning and predicting decisions that are arising or should be advancing on agendas. More importantly, the evidence shows that a re-imagined institutional research function will be essential to meeting the challenges facing higher education in a rapidly changing landscape."—*Randy L. Swing, Independent Consultant*

Student Affairs by the Numbers

Quantitative Research and Statistics for Professionals

Rishi Sriram

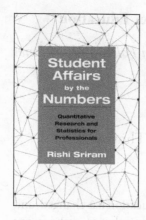

"Rishi Sriram's philosophical approach to research and the phobia surrounding statistical analysis is spot on. Students will find great value in reading this book, as will professionals working on their institution's accreditation. Perhaps the greatest value the book provides is setting the tone for developing and sustaining a culture of research and assessment."—*Matthew R. Wawrzynski, Associate Professor and Coordinator Higher, Adult, and Lifelong Education Program, Michigan State University; Executive Editor,* Journal of Student Affairs Research and Practice

"*Student Affairs by the Numbers* couldn't arrive at a better time. The pressure from state-based performance-based funding, increased rigor from regional accrediting agencies, and an increase in a 'return-on-investment' approach to funding and program review underscores the critical importance of developing a core competence in quantitative statistics and assessment. This book is a valuable resource for student affairs professionals and graduate students who are developing research and evaluation efforts on core student affairs programs and services."—*Kevin Kruger, President of NASPA–Student Affairs Administrators in Higher Education*

The Science of Higher Education

State Higher Education Policy and the Laws of Scale

Mario C. Martinez

Foreword by Scott L. Thomas

From the Foreword:

"The context of higher education has changed, and Martinez is no longer content with incremental approaches to evolving our thinking and work in higher education finance. Adapting methods used to model dynamic systems, he offers scale analysis as a new way of capturing public benefits. . . . Throughout the book, Martinez provides a wealth of examples, analyses, and comparisons to demonstrate this approach's utility. While admittedly oversimplified, his approach does represent a genuine shift in our paradigm—one that is likely to cause discomfort and controversy among many in the field.

Do the contents of this book constitute the beginning of a *Science of Higher Education*? I leave that to the reader to decide. Regardless of your opinion on that count, I hope you will agree that this book offers more science than this area has seen since Berdahl and his contemporaries laid the foundation of our current knowledge base in the 1970s."—**Scott L. Thomas**, *Professor and Dean, College of Education and Social Services—University of Vermont*

Digital Leadership in Higher Education

Purposeful Social Media in a Connected World

Josie Ahlquist

"*Digital Leadership in Higher Education: Purposeful Social Media in a Connected World* is a timely and relevant book given the global pandemic's impact on the necessity of leaders to have an online presence. The purpose of this book is to serve as a resource for leaders in higher education who want to purposefully engage with social media platforms as part of their leadership approach. Ahlquist. . . skillfully walk[s] readers through the tensions that reside at the intersection of the purpose of social media within the context of higher education, the theory of digital leadership, and the practice of digital leadership by higher education leaders.

The book seems to be targeted to an audience of higher education professionals who are cautious, skeptical, late, or laggard adopters of social media and technology. Although addressed to senior administrators, the book could be valuable for faculty professional developments to offer training on connecting with students in online environments.

Student affairs/ higher education graduate preparation programs should use this book in leadership courses to grapple with digital leadership in practice. In summary, [this] is a timely and relevant book to prompt a reimagining of leadership in the digital age of connection."—*Teachers College Record*

Also available from Stylus

Managing Your Professional Identity Online

A Guide for Faculty, Staff, and Administrators

Kathryn E. Linder

Foreword by Laura Pasquini

"*Managing Your Professional Identity Online* is pragmatic, practical, and offers an important set of tools and questions for academics to consider regarding online networked practices. The strength is the way the text provides a broad overview of a range of issues related to the development and management of an academic identity online. Linder covers a variety of topics – from the range of platforms and tools—to issues around accessibility, management, and knowledge of content creation and community building—that are important for higher education professionals in the digital age."—*Paul Eaton, Assistant Professor, Department of Educational Leadership, Sam Houston State University*

"I found *Managing Your Professional Identity Online* to be a practical and compelling guide for building an online professional brand. This text pulls together the technical experience with the why and how-to of building an online professional presence and is a much-needed resource in the field. It fills a unique niche that has needed a publication like this."—*Jennifer H. Herman, Director, Center for Excellence in Teaching, Simmons College*

22883 Quicksilver Drive
Sterling, VA 20166-2019   Subscribe to our e-mail alerts: www.Styluspub.com